"Megan Salar's revolutionary, effective work in eye movement desensitization and reprocessing (EMDR) is brought to life in this extraordinary workbook. Pouring her unique years of experience in the field and her remarkable, hard-won insight into trauma and recovery, Salar gifts readers with stories that decrease isolation as she spells out potent life skills to manage triggers, and delivers on her promise to take your life back! A profoundly powerful leap forward for victims of trauma."

—**Bridget Cook-Burch**, *New York Times* and *Wall Street Journal* bestselling author of *The Witness Wore Red*, cofounder of www.sheroesunited.org, and CEO of www.yourinspiredstory.com

"Warm, friendly, and thorough. Using this workbook feels like having your own caring, personal mentor guiding you on your journey from victim to victor. I highly recommend it to anyone wishing to make more out of their life. It is an excellent self-help guide, and so encouraging. How I wish it had been available to me and my clients before I retired."

—**Gail B. Anderson, MCoun**, BIS, Brigham Young University, director of Direction Inc., counseling, training, and consulting, EMDR, NLP, self-hypnosis trainer

"*The EMDR Workbook for Trauma and PTSD* is innovative, authentic, and relevant. Megan Salar serves as a guide for you as you walk through your own journey in finding peace from your past and hope for your future. Megan's voice is full of grit, determination, and fortitude as she introduces each chapter with the inspirational stories of her real-life heroes who have healed through the power of EMDR. This book has restored my faith in what resources are out there for survivors, and serves as a gift for those who may not be ready or able to tackle traditional therapy."

—**Alexis Amrein**, mental health case manager, CBRS worker, and child advocate

The
EMDR
Workbook for
Trauma & PTSD

Skills to Manage Triggers,
Move Beyond Traumatic Memories
& Take Back Your Life

MEGAN SALAR, LCSW

New Harbinger Publications, Inc.

Publisher's Note

This publication is designed to provide accurate and authoritative information in regard to the subject matter covered. It is sold with the understanding that the publisher is not engaged in rendering psychological, financial, legal, or other professional services. If expert assistance or counseling is needed, the services of a competent professional should be sought.

NEW HARBINGER PUBLICATIONS is a registered trademark of New Harbinger Publications, Inc.

New Harbinger Publications is an employee-owned company.

Copyright © 2022 by Megan Salar

New Harbinger Publications, Inc.
5720 Shattuck Avenue
Oakland, CA 94609
www.newharbinger.com

Cover design by Amy Shoup

Acquired by Ryan Buresh

Edited by Rona Bernstein

Library of Congress Cataloging-in-Publication Data on file

Printed in the United States of America

26   25   24

10   9   8   7   6   5   4   3

*For Jordan P. You are the real-life Wonder Woman and one of the most valiant individuals
I have ever come to know. Thank you for inspiring me and so many others with your relentless spirit.*

Contents

Foreword

A healing journey is often described as a long and winding road, one full of twists and turns. Along the way, it is helpful to have a skilled guide whose purpose is to help you feel less alone and who helps you navigate the inner terrain that may still feel devastated by traumatic events. While a therapist is an essential source of this wise guidance, it is common to also seek additional support, especially between sessions. I can recall my own longing for such guidance when I began EMDR therapy many years ago to heal from my own wounds. How comforting it would have been to have Megan Salar's workbook to accompany me and help me understand that the vulnerable feelings I was having were completely normal. Now, over twenty years later, I can confidently say that EMDR changed my life and inspired me to become a therapist, trainer, and consultant guiding countless others through this transformational approach to healing.

When I first met Megan, we both felt an immediate sense of connection and recognition that we shared the same values regarding the role of EMDR therapy in trauma recovery. We both value the necessity of adapting this modality to meet the needs and pace of the individual. We both recognize that all good therapy relies upon feeling safe enough to heal. Together, we believe in resilience and the human capacity to overcome adversities so long as we have sufficient support. Having this book by your side will undoubtedly be a voice of comfort during times in which a dark night feels frightening or lonely. When you have a history of trauma, you might experience intrusive thoughts or flashbacks in which distressing images or emotions feel overwhelming. What is often challenging during these times is that the skills and resources you may have learned from your therapist are more difficult to remember or practice. It is at these very moments that you can reach for this book and Megan will lovingly guide you back to a sense of ease and inner calm. She will invite you to set aside your self-critic and embrace yourself in a loving and caring manner. Moreover, you now have at your fingertips access to practical instructions that will help you feel grounded and back on your healing path.

Resilience is grounded in an understanding that we have the ability to work through difficult feelings of terror, rage, shame, and despair and that in doing so, we can ultimately discover a greater sense of wisdom, strength, freedom, and peace. When you are climbing a mountain, you will not arrive at the top without effort. However, when you have the right resources in place, such as a good map, the right shoes, enough water, and hiking poles, you can ultimately stand at the summit because you had support and you didn't give up. Likewise, your journey requires that you have access to resources and that you proceed mindfully, taking one step at a time.

Resilience isn't something that you are simply born with; rather, it involves cultivating beneficial thoughts and behaviors that you can repeatedly practice. The tools of resilience involve cultivating self-compassion, courageously feeling and working through difficult emotions from the past, and developing your capacity to visualize the future you long to create. By practicing these skills you will enhance your ability not only to handle adversity but also to grow as a result of your commitment to your healing journey. As you build your resilience, you will find that you are better able to navigate the obstacles that arise as part of this complex, human world we share. We are all faced with challenges in life; however, you can strengthen your capacity to navigate these inevitable stressors with a greater sense of internal steadiness and equanimity.

It takes great courage to stay open to a world that has been a source of pain, hurt, or betrayal. You hold in your hands a book that will undoubtedly serve as a source of comfort and hope during any rocky moments that you may face as you navigate your healing journey with EMDR therapy. Return again and again, for it is through the repeated practice of these healing tools that you will discover the unwavering and profound strength that you carry within you.

—Arielle Schwartz, PhD
Clinical psychologist, EMDR trainer, and author of six books
focused on trauma recovery including *The Complex PTSD Workbook*
and *EMDR Therapy and Somatic Psychology.*

Introduction

You are fierce. You're a survivor. You're a fighter through and through.
Little brave, breathe. There is a warrior within you.

—Beau Taplin

You are never alone in your pain. Never. These words can be hard to fully believe, and at times I still struggle to believe them myself. You may live in a broken world, as many of us do, where life is messy, hurtful, and confusing, and at times the pain is consuming. The suffering you experience may seem so vast and heavy that it feels insurmountable. You may wonder if you will ever be able to find the peace you are searching for. And you may feel alone—alone in the way you respond and struggle with things, alone in the pain, alone in the shame, alone in your intense stress, alone in your fear. And you may believe that you are the only one who must feel or experience life this way. You may even believe that no one could relate to or accept you if they knew the demons you carry within.

Does the pain you hold feel as if you are thrashing in a storm of wreckage? The waves seem one hundred feet tall and crashing all around you. Among the waves, it makes sense that you cannot see all the other survivors struggling with their own waves of pain, wreckage, and hopelessness. I want you to know, even if you don't believe this yet, that you already are a survivor. There are many survivors like you waiting to be connected, healed, and brought together. Trust me. I have thrashed through many waves of my own, believing that I too was alone and lost forever. By reading this book, you are starting a healing journey that includes becoming a life raft for yourself and so many others desperate to find and connect with survivors like you.

We're in This Together

We can find each other in likely, or unlikely, places. You found me through this book, and during a summer job in college I found fellow survivors at a residential treatment facility for adolescent boys. This was a very unlikely place for me, and definitely my last option for summer work, as all the boys in this facility had lengthy juvenile records, substance abuse issues, and severe mental health concerns. I doubted my ability to serve them, as I had never touched a drug in my life, had only ever gotten a speeding ticket, and had avoided criminal activity to focus on being an athlete. How could I become a life raft in these storms of life that I knew nothing about? Little did I know, that summer would change my life.

I soon came to realize that the drugs and criminality that coated these boys were merely masks hiding and protecting their deepest wounds; they clung to the masks in order to survive. I recognized the pain, trauma, abandonment, fear, loneliness, broken dreams, and sheer survival of these boys because I personally knew it all very well. These same experiences had been haunting me from my earliest memories. I had different masks of survival than theirs, but under the masks for us both were flashbacks, nightmares, and repetitive thoughts of fear, blame, and doubt. While I had learned how to adapt, use my athletic abilities to fit in, and avoid the pain that lingered in my home and the inner workings of my mind, I began to see myself in these boys. I envied their courage and raw ability to act out and speak their truth, no matter how messy and chaotic. In some ways, I even envied them because of the help they were receiving, as it felt unattainable to me.

These boys spoke my language and I spoke theirs. Not with drugs or acting out, but through a deep aching that few take the time to recognize. We understood despair. I knew how to relate to their desperate tactics of survival. Most importantly, I noticed the lost child in the corner, isolated and alone—for I had been that child. Seeing my own buried reality mirrored back to me through these boys finally allowed me the opportunity to step in and do what I had longed for someone to do for me. I did the only things I knew how to do at that time: Accept them. Notice them. Listen. Support them. Hold firm but loving boundaries. Treat them according to the potential they each carried, rather than limit them to the mistakes they had made. We all want these things and to be seen this way, as they create hope. The experience was heart-wrenching and lit a fire in my soul. I changed my major from sports management to psychology and set out to become a therapist. While the pain of those boys, like mine, stemmed from traumatic childhood experiences, my life's mission—and the aim of this book—is to help people who have experienced any type of trauma in their life, whether it be abuse, violence, devastating accidents, war, natural disasters, or other traumatic experiences.

Everyone deserves to be fought for, to have a place where they feel safe, to be seen for who they really are—not judged or chained by their past experiences. We all deserve a place where we can be supported, healed, and feel life returned to us. Know this: no matter what type of trauma you have experienced, and what pain you have faced, there are people and places that will support, love, and empower you more than you ever thought possible. We're in this together.

The Distinction Between Trauma and PTSD

Posttraumatic stress disorder (PTSD) has become a common diagnosis over the last several decades. While we often think of trauma and PTSD similarly, it's important to understand the difference between them. We all experience varying degrees of trauma, which we can refer to as an event that has negatively impacted our lives in some shape or form.

PTSD, on the other hand, is a clinical disorder that is diagnosed by a licensed mental health practitioner. It occurs when the effects of trauma linger and cause severe emotional, social, and mental distress for a long period of time. The impact of the trauma leads to re-experiencing it through nightmares, flashbacks, thoughts, or sensory reminders, as well as repeated attempts to avoid thoughts, feelings, and reminders of the traumatic event(s). Other aspects of PTSD include negative changes in thoughts, mood, and emotions (e.g., feeling isolated and detached from others; blaming oneself; having negative beliefs about oneself, others, or the world; experiencing persistent negative emotions) and noticeable differences in one's reactions to situations (e.g., being hypervigilant, startling easily, having difficulty concentrating or sleeping, having angry outbursts).

If you've been diagnosed with PTSD or wonder if you suffer from the impact of trauma alone or PTSD, I would encourage you to talk to a mental health professional who is "trauma-informed" and can adequately assist you in screening and diagnosis. While some of you may meet the criteria for PTSD and some of you may not, please know that regardless of your diagnosis, your story and your experiences matter. In this book, I will be referring to both PTSD and trauma to assist you in overcoming whatever experiences you have faced.

Survival and the Longing to Feel Fully Alive

Survival is ingrained into your being. You are an expert in your own survival guide of life. You are familiar with your own devastating, difficult, earth-shattering events that have required you to endure hardships, often with no other choice and likely a lot of numbness. Most certainly you have endured these events with indescribable pain. The root of the word "survivor" comes from the Latin word *vivere*, which simply means "to live." The prefix "sur" means "to rise over or above." If we combine these parts, we have a new definition of the word "survive": to rise over and above something and keep on living.

What would it take for you to rise over your pain and struggles to truly keep living? Please don't think that to keep living means simply enduring. Rather, I want you to imagine what it would feel like to actually be "alive." Alive with hope. Alive with confidence. Alive with peace. And most importantly, alive within yourself—giving you the ability to rise above and embrace your life to the fullest.

On this journey, we can hit stumbling blocks to feeling fully alive. As a therapist, I have continued forward with a purposeful blueprint of healing myself and others, but there have been barriers—a lot of them. I tell you this because you need to know that challenges, heartache, and growing pains are part of the path to healing. Over my years as a psychotherapist, I have witnessed a common cycle emerge among those of us who wrestle with trying to overcome our past trauma, whether or not we are diagnosed with PTSD. Many of my clients have gone through years of psychotherapy, medication, energy work, self-help books, and so on, longing for that sense of aliveness, only to find themselves writhing with memories, painful emotional reactions, and episodes of debilitating depression or anxiety that seem to never fully subside, leading to the conclusion that they are doomed to a life of suffering.

As a seasoned clinician, the more I began to see my clients experience these barriers of change, the more I knew that something was missing in the treatment and understanding of trauma and more specifically PTSD. I was eventually introduced to a method called eye movement desensitization and reprocessing (EMDR), which was developed by Francine Shapiro beginning in 1987 (Shapiro 2018). I had stumbled across EMDR almost a decade earlier but couldn't quite accept the idea that eye movements could somehow help heal the lingering effects of PTSD. At the time, it was still heavily debated in the counseling world, and I wondered if clients would buy into this type of nontraditional therapy. As I continued to research and explore its effectiveness, I learned that EMDR is in fact scientifically based and highly evidence-based.

In fact, EMDR has been found to be effective in treating PTSD and many other mental health disorders, such as substance use disorders, depression, anxiety, and somatic (i.e., bodily) issues. EMDR has become one of the leading treatment approaches for PTSD worldwide and is recognized by the World Health Organization, the Department of Veteran Affairs, and others as a leader in trauma and PTSD treatment modalities (Eye Movement Desensitization and Reprocessing International Association 2022). As I learned more, I began to understand EMDR's ability to rapidly heal and reduce symptoms associated with trauma. I wondered if this would be the answer I had been searching for that could restore hope and healing.

It took one session of my own with an EMDR therapist to realize the power of this method. The relief I experienced from just one session was astounding. It left me feeling alive. I was empowered and curious to learn more so I could share this with others.

Over the years of receiving extensive training and providing EMDR to clients, I have made this the focal point of my practice. I have seen countless lives changed and healed in ways that could not be achieved through traditional therapy. It will take your own personal experience to understand just how effective EMDR can be, and I hope that this workbook will give you the same healing and hope for life that I, along with so many others, have found through this work.

Through this workbook, you will learn ways to rise above any limitation you may have from your past. If this is difficult to believe, allow me to carry the hope for you until you can arrive at this conclusion for yourself, and trust me, you will.

How EMDR Works with PTSD and Trauma

Your past experiences shape your brain's many memory networks and teach you how to respond (whether positively or negatively) in future situations. Your belief system, self-esteem, and self-worth are also directly formed from these past experiences (Shapiro 2018).

Yet the idea of change and exposing your pain can feel damning or hopeless. The fear of reliving these past memories and emotions can keep you constricted in your day-to-day life. Maybe you don't even know how or what to do to confront them. This is where EMDR comes in. It enables you to put to rest the painful emotional intensity of your negative past experiences. EMDR allows your brain to process your memories associated with past traumatic events by decreasing your brain's response to unnecessary triggers. It enables distressing memories and sensations to get unstuck in the brain so that they no longer rule your life or thoughts (Shapiro 2018). Think of it as a technique that jump-starts your brain's natural healing process.

In this book, I will help you learn how to use EMDR skills to confront your trauma. You will gain clarity on your past experiences, learn about the nature of your perceptions and fears, and gain insight into the subconscious survival techniques that you have been clinging to in order to preserve yourself emotionally and physically.

EMDR was founded and researched using eye movements that mimicked our REM (rapid eye movements) during sleep. Many studies have shown that during the REM sleep cycle, your eyes move from right to left under your eyelids very rapidly. Research involving brain scans, sleep studies, and other methods has shown that during the REM cycle of sleep, your brain filters the experiences it had during the day. It stores what is useful (positive memories like an engagement or birthday) and discards what is meaningless (the outfit we wore to work or the drive home in the car). The REM cycle also allows the brain's natural healing process to engage and help the brain repair itself.

Traumatic memories tend to get stuck in our brain and are stored in their own trauma memory network. Researchers found that if they used the same natural healing process that occurs during REM, while focusing on a traumatic memory, the brain will be able to access, process, and resolve these memories. Research has shown that EMDR helps your brain resolve upsetting memories, lowers your stress level, increases insight, improves self-worth and self-esteem, restores confidence, and allows the brain to function more wholly. This process allows for a decrease in PTSD symptoms (Shapiro 2018).

Although EMDR was first developed using eye movements, ongoing research and continued clinical findings have shown that a variety of *bilateral stimulation* methods (stimulating the right, then left side of the body, which is similar to what happens during REM) are just as effective as eye movements. In chapter three, you will learn four options for bilateral stimulation that access the brain's natural healing process. You can choose from among them and use what you feel most comfortable with as you do the exercises throughout this workbook.

The techniques drawn from EMDR in this workbook can help you address past experiences, understand and manage current triggers, and assist you with facing future anticipated challenges. By working with the past, present, and future (called a three-prong approach in EMDR), you will open new pathways in your brain that have been closed off or constricted. Your brain will be able to properly store what is useful in a way that is healing, helpful, and positive.

Things to Remember

Before we begin, it's important to point out that the evidence-based tools, tips, and techniques taught in this book are most useful in conjunction with doing your own therapeutic work with a licensed professional; this workbook does not replace EMDR therapy. As such, I encourage you to find a certified EMDR therapist who can assist you along your journey while you do this work. The effectiveness of EMDR is based on working with a trained and certified EMDR therapist. A list of certified EMDR therapists can be found at https://www.emdria.org.

It is also important to note that the exercises in this workbook are not guaranteed to be effective for everyone and can be upsetting given that the nature of the content is based around trauma and highly distressing events. If you experience an increase in symptoms, please use caution and discontinue if it feels to be too much. It is important that you have access to positive support and resources. You can find a resource list on the website for this book, http://www.newharbinger.com/49586. (See the very back of this book for more details.) If you feel you need more support as you do the exercises in this workbook, please allow yourself to ask for help or give yourself permission to take a break. It is important to pay attention to your needs, honor your experiences, and ask for help. Self-care will always be critical to your healing.

I hope this workbook will lead you to your own EMDR testament of healing. Right now, you are starting your own courageous path to healing. I have no doubt that as you continue to learn and grow through this workbook of EMDR strategies—hopefully while also working with an EMDR therapist—you will come to believe that healing can be attained and that change is possible.

Choose to hear me when I say that this work you are about to do matters. Your story matters. And you matter more than you even realize. Thank you for joining me on this healing path and allowing me to be a guide on your journey.

CHAPTER ONE

Prepare for Your Healing Journey

The wilderness is where all the creatives and prophets and system-buckers and risk-takers have always lived, and it is stunningly vibrant. The walk out there is hard, but the authenticity out there is life.

—Brené Brown, *Braving the Wilderness*

Let's make a commitment, right from the start, that you will be all in for yourself during this journey. As we move toward approaching your pain and suffering, I know it will be difficult, and your gut reaction may be to want to avoid or justify not facing these emotions. Those feelings are completely normal. You will do anything you can to protect yourself from the past pain that you have experienced; we all do this—it is innate survival at its finest. The memories and thoughts of past trauma can seem retraumatizing, and your natural reaction will no doubt be to avoid this pain.

If you have invested in this book, I am assuming that you have come to a place where you recognize that the pain stays with you whether you face it or leave it buried within yourself. And your choice to be where you are right now, reading this, tells me that you desire to heal and move past the hurt. If that is the case, I have good news: you will indeed begin to learn the skills and tools necessary to face these things and move past them.

Moving *past* something requires us to first move *through* something. If we do not learn how to navigate through our difficulties, we face the risk of staying stagnant and continuing to suffer silently. Being present, here and now, means that you are already on your way to the movement and change you seek.

Take a moment to reflect on and write down what you are hoping to heal and move past. Note anything that comes to mind.

_____

_____

_____

_____

_____

_____

_____

Commend yourself for being brave enough to start facing what you just reflected upon. The resiliency that shows will help you as you continue moving along your path of healing.

In this chapter, I will help you begin developing a new perspective and understanding of your trauma. Then I will introduce new ways to be introspective, compassionate, and nonjudgmental toward yourself and the struggles you have faced. I'll encourage you to continue taking steps forward on your path as you begin to rediscover your purpose and learn how to tap into your creativity through the use of your imagination. Along the way, you will be reminded of the power of your mind and your own resiliency. First, let's deepen our understanding of what trauma and PTSD are.

The Misunderstanding of Trauma and PTSD

Whether you have experienced abuse, violence, sexual assault, war, natural disaster, racism, the traumatic death of a loved one, or situations less typically thought of as trauma (like betrayal, bullying, or divorce), the struggles you have faced are unique to you as an individual. Trauma impacts all of us in our own way; we all have our own unique fingerprint of trauma.

There are times when trauma and its indicators are misunderstood—even within the mental health profession. Unfortunately when this occurs, your symptoms of trauma or PTSD may continue to go untreated, resulting in ongoing struggles. This can leave you feeling frustrated, hopeless, and fearful that you will never find relief.

When trauma and PTSD are not screened for properly, people are commonly misdiagnosed with conditions such as bipolar disorder, depression, anxiety, attention deficit/hyperactivity disorder (ADHD), and borderline personality disorder, among others. For example, you may have difficulty concentrating, be on edge, and have racing thoughts, all of which could align with ADHD or anxiety. However, it is common for individuals who have experienced trauma to be unable to focus or maintain clarity and to lack a sense of peace, which can result in similar symptoms to those described above. Although these diagnoses are not always inaccurate, it is important for you to know that trauma and PTSD can resemble and overlap with other mental health conditions. When trauma is recognized, understood, acknowledged, and properly treated, many of these symptoms can and will improve.

Mark some of the symptoms on this list that you notice affecting you today. Be aware that this is not a list of symptoms of PTSD (although many are), but rather a list of experiences common among people who have experienced trauma.

- ☐ Denying the impact of your experiences

- ☐ Doubting/questioning if what happened to you was real

- ☐ Difficulty managing/controlling your feelings/emotions (e.g., anger, sadness, shame)

- ☐ Difficulty identifying or understanding your emotions

- ☐ Difficulty identifying or pinpointing why you get upset or reactive

- ☐ Sense of "losing it"

- ☐ Compulsive behaviors/self-medicating (e.g., substance abuse, overeating, overspending)

- ☐ Feeling too much or too little

- ☐ Frequent feelings of detachment or being "checked out"

- ☐ Somatic (physical) symptoms that cannot be better explained by something else

- ☐ Frequently on edge and anxious or worried

- ☐ Sleep disturbances

- ☐ Intrusive thoughts of past negative experiences or memories

- ☐ Feeling different from others

- ☐ Avoiding anything that reminds you of the past or provokes anxiety

- ☐ Difficulty trusting others

- ☐ Intense fear or feelings of helplessness

As you consider some of your own symptoms, I want you to know that you are not alone, different, broken, or damaged. You have merely endured situations and circumstances that have left your brain in a state of survival. These reactions are your brain's way of preparing you to react and avoid future anticipated threats or danger. I will help you understand how and why your brain has interpreted these experiences in the way that it has and assist you in learning ways to manage these reactions when they occur. Consider some questions.

1. Have you ever felt that you have been misdiagnosed or misunderstood? How has this affected you?

    _____

    _____

    _____

2. In what ways have you mislabeled or misunderstood your own symptoms or responses?

    _____

    _____

    _____

3. What are some ways that understanding your own symptoms of trauma or PTSD will help you heal and empower you to continue forward on your journey?

    _____

    _____

    _____

    _____

    _____

How Your Brain Responds to Trauma

Now let's turn to how and why your brain responds and reacts when you have experienced trauma. To simplify the idea of how your brain works, you can think of the brain in terms of a stoplight. You have a green light, yellow light, and red light that help your brain to operate accordingly. Just like a traffic light, each of these lights, or parts of the brain, has a different function. The front part of your brain, the cortex, is what I refer to as your "green light." Its role is to make sure everything is operating smoothly—that you feel safe and can use logic, weigh pros and cons, and make clear-headed decisions. This "green light" also helps you to sift through emotions, problem solve, and brainstorm.

The mid part of your brain, or the "yellow light" region, is part of the amygdala. The amygdala is responsible for assessing if we are in danger and determines if we should react or if we are safe and can relax. The amygdala assists you with processing emotions and ultimately determines how you will respond. It has frequently been referred to by many in the field, including Bessel van der Kolk, as the smoke detector of the brain. The amygdala is also responsible for aspects of our memory bank and plays a key role in attaching emotions to related memories. If we experience a particular emotion, depending on the type of feeling we have, the amygdala will either flood us with positive sensations or remind us of past painful experiences.

In addition to calling it the yellow light part of the brain, I have also found it helpful to liken the amygdala to a person—I even named her Amy. Just as a yellow light tells you to use caution and be on the lookout for danger, Amy's sole job in your brain is to constantly assess and look out for harm. She is kind of like that person in your life who remembers *everything* and never lets anything go. In fact, she is so worrisome and has such an exceptional memory that she can recall every sight, taste, touch, sound, and smell from every past experience you have ever had. And, should she perceive even just one sensation that was familiar to a past negative event you experienced, she will react instantly, telling your brain that you are potentially in danger.

For example, let's say you are driving in a car and as you are crossing an intersection while listening to Garth Brooks on the radio, suddenly you are T-boned out of nowhere and succumb to a concussion and a few broken ribs. Years later, you are on a road trip with some friends and that same Garth Brooks song that was playing when you were T-boned comes on the radio. Instantly your heart begins to race, you recall details of that incident, and you feel tense. This is because Amy remembers this incident and her job is to help assess for safety and prepare you for action. She only needs one small detail, memory, or sensation to instantly respond and tell your brain that you are not safe and should prepare for action. And just as a traffic light goes from yellow to red, Amy can quickly initiate the red light part of your brain should she feel threatened or reminded of past trauma.

Just like a traffic light, a green light and red light cannot both go off at the same time. So when the "red light," or back part, of your brain is triggered, the front part (i.e., green light) of your brain, which is responsible for problem solving, brainstorming, and making rational decisions, goes offline and you are left with only your basic survival responses: fight, flight, or freeze (i.e., red light). This is a hardwired survival response that is fully intact when you are born, ensuring your survival from the time you are an infant. In contrast, the green light region and all the other parts of your brain take approximately twenty-two years to fully develop. In order for these parts to develop to their full potential and be utilized in the way that they were intended, they require positive experiences, secure attachments, and feelings of physical and emotional safety.

Your Senses and Trauma Triggers

Now let's deepen your knowledge of the brain even further so that you can recognize how your senses are also involved in this process as they take in information from your surroundings. Your five senses and the sensory input that your brain receives from each of your senses are main players in your brain's process of determining if it is safe or in danger. Many people do not understand how or why they are so easily triggered by their sensory experiences. You may assume, like many do, that in order to be triggered you must encounter a similar experience to that which was once traumatic for you. However, when trauma occurs, the brain actually is more concerned about storing the specific sensory details (e.g., smells, sounds, physical sensations, sight) of the event than the experience itself. This occurs so that the next time your brain encounters *any* of these previous sensations that were once connected to a trauma, your brain can react, respond, and keep you safe.

Take a moment to identify which sensations cause you the most distress. Circle yes or no for the sensations and triggers you notice most frequently.

Sight: Are there certain things that you see (e.g., colors, objects, places, people) that elicit strong physical or emotional responses?

Circle: YES   NO

If yes, what are they? _____

_____

Sound: Are there noises, frequencies, or tones that disrupt you to the point of feeling hypervigilant, anxious, or unnerved?

Circle: YES   NO

If yes, what are they? _____

_____

Do you tend to notice noises and sounds that others seem to miss or not be startled by?

Circle: YES   NO

Smell: Are there specific smells that you cannot stand or that lead you to recall past unpleasant events in your life?

Circle: YES   NO

If yes, what are they? _____

_____

Touch: Are there particular physical sensations or certain types of touch that startle you or make you feel uneasy, uncomfortable, tense, or reactive?

Circle: YES   NO

If yes, what are they? _____

_____

Taste: Are there types of textures or individual tastes that elicit physical responses of disgust or trigger unwanted memories?

Circle: YES   NO

If yes, what are they? _____

_____

As you are coming to understand the way your brain responds to sensory input it receives, consider some of your own sensory reactions that may be related to your trauma or PTSD and that you may have overlooked or downplayed. The greater your insight becomes, the easier it will be to recognize, manage, and control your feelings and behaviors. On the website for this book, http://www.newharbinger.com/49586, you'll find an audio recording of a guided body scan exercise. Learning to "tune in" to your body and its messages will take some practice, but the results will lead to a more balanced you!

Your Physical Symptoms

In addition to these sensory reactions, you may experience behavioral and physical symptoms related to trauma that you were unaware of. In the space provided, draw a simple picture of a person with their whole body (it can be as simple as a stick figure) and imagine this being your own body. Once you have completed the drawing, circle, color, or identify all the places where you notice your symptoms. For example:

- Do you need to draw a box on your stomach because you often feel tightness there?

- Maybe you need to scribble on your shoulders because they become tense and hold a lot of anxiety.

- Perhaps draw a line through your chest because it feels sharp. Or if at times you sense a certain heaviness there, color it gray.

There is no right or wrong way to do this activity. What is most important is considering and increasing your awareness of how your body responds and reacts to trauma and emotions.

The parts of your body that you identified in your picture can demonstrate how your own sub-conscious sensory information leads to behavioral and physical reactions. Your brain and body are closely intertwined and work together as a means of keeping you safe. In addition to storing and interpreting these emotional and physical sensations, your brain also assigns meaning to each scenario that you face throughout your life.

The cool thing about your brain is that it has the ability to change—to rewire and reprocess things in new ways and give your past new meaning. This means that even Amy can learn to let go of things she once saw as harmful and that it's no longer necessary to carry such burdens.

1. How different would it feel, or how might your life be different, if you were able to manage your physical and emotional symptoms so they didn't interfere as much?

    _____

    _____

    _____

2. How do you feel knowing that your brain has the ability to change and relearn things? Does this feel hard? Does it give you hope? Are you feeling curious to know more?

    _____

    _____

    _____

3. If you no longer had to carry the weight of your own trauma or feel so caught off guard by your responses, how might your life change?

    _____

    _____

    _____

When your symptoms are triggered, you often assume it has something to do with your immediate environment. You may believe at that moment that you are helpless and in danger. You may be powerless over your thoughts in the moment due to the way your brain is hardwired to respond, but you are not helpless—you are just trying to survive. Becoming more aware of your body will help you deepen your understanding of yourself and potentially lead to lessening the physical stress your body experiences.

On the website for this book (http://www.newharbinger.com/49586), you will find a Trauma Symptoms Checklist, which will help you identify your emotional, psychological, and physical symptoms of trauma. I recommend that you visit the website and complete the checklist. In order for true healing to begin, it is important for you to increase your awareness of some of the symptoms you are experiencing that are related to trauma.

Laying Down the Burden of Self-Judgment

Do not doubt your own ability to heal. Believe in your resilience; it has been there all along and has helped lead you to where you are today, even it has been messy along the way. No matter how big or small or different your experiences feel from other people's or how many times you have been told that you should just get over it or not react the way you do, if these experiences disrupt you, they deserve time and attention. They deserve to be grieved, honored, understood, and healed. It is easy to fall victim to comparison and to minimize your own trauma or PTSD symptoms and experiences.

You may hear stories more grave or unfathomable than yours and wonder how the "small things" that you wrestle with can even hold significance. I have worked with many clients over the years who have experienced devastating situations. One in particular described her upbringing of being sexually abused by her father, having her fingertips burned until they blistered as a punishment for playing with lighters, being physically abused countless times to the point of bleeding and bruising, and having a constant fear of not knowing what to expect. As she described these incidents, she would commonly refer to them as being "normal." She never knew any different until she finally learned that these acts of violence were tragic and traumatic. Even when you have experienced earth-shattering trauma, you may still have the tendency to doubt or downplay your experiences and numb yourself to avoid any more pain for sheer survival. Or you may, like the client above, question what is wrong with you and how so many others with the same problems, or worse, seem to be coping just fine. I want you to learn to surrender your comparison to others' experiences. I want you to free yourself from the judgment that you carry of yourself and begin to be compassionate toward yourself. What has happened to you matters, even if you think it doesn't matter to the rest of the world.

As you begin to uncover the root causes of many of your symptoms, you will find that your reactions are in fact normal. Anyone who has faced the circumstances that you have would respond in ways that are uncharacteristic of their nature. The good news is that once you identify what triggers these responses, you can start to build skills to proactively manage these symptoms in your life.

Let's work together to start releasing your self-judgment. This will help you begin to minimize your isolation, loneliness, and negative thoughts and feelings. First, we need to look at your specific pattern of self-judgment.

What are some ways in which you judge or minimize yourself or compare yourself to others? Check the boxes that apply to you.

☐ You find yourself frequently comparing your experiences to others'.

☐ You minimize or downplay the painful experiences you have faced.

☐ You believe that the negative events in your life were your fault.

☐ You are very hard on yourself and hold yourself to higher expectations than others in your life.

☐ You struggle to forgive yourself or move past mistakes you have made.

☐ You believe that you are too sensitive or emotionally reactive and that others are more emotionally stable than you.

☐ You are down on yourself as a person and see yourself falling short when compared to others.

☐ You feel a great deal of shame for the things you have endured in your life.

☐ You chronically feel like there is something wrong with you and assume that others are coping or managing life better than you.

☐ You lack confidence in your ability to make decisions and to make changes.

In order for you to surrender the self-judgment and tendency to compare yourself with others, you must first learn how to change the way you relate to yourself.

Reconnecting to Yourself

Connecting to yourself requires vulnerability, trust, and exploration. You may be asking what I mean by "connection." Let me explain. Connection is your ability to be aware of your feelings, behaviors, reactions, and physical sensations. It is your ability to tune in to yourself in a nonjudgmental, compassionate manner. And in relation to others it is your ability to be vulnerable, transparent, and present with those closest to you. Connection requires us to relate rather than compare ourselves and gives us a sense of security that we are in fact not alone.

The antidote to your pain starts with connection: Connection to love. Connection to forgiveness. Connection to vulnerability. Connection to honesty. Connection to support. Connection to your authentic, real self. Connection to those who are able to see you for your strength and capabilities.

Take a moment and reflect on what connection means to you. *Connection to myself means:*

_____

_____

_____

Describe the most important part of yourself that you would like to learn to feel more love and connection toward.

_____

_____

_____

_____

_____

_____

I would like to challenge you to tune in, every day, to this part of yourself that you just identified. This can simply be by noticing how judgmental you have been toward yourself, or identifying some way to show yourself appreciation, or perhaps even by journaling about the part of yourself that feels judged and needs more compassion. Whatever you choose, just be intentional in your efforts to connect with this important part of your unique being.

As you do this, give yourself permission to just be curious. Maintaining curiosity about yourself will help you as you work toward increasing your self-compassion. You have likely judged yourself hard enough already. When you choose to be curious and give yourself compassion, you will find that you are able not only to truly connect but also to heal the traumatic parts of yourself that you have struggled to understand.

Write down some things you are curious about. What do you want to know more about?

I am curious about these feelings: _____

_____

_____

I am curious about these experiences from my past: _____

_____

_____

I am curious about these habits: _____

_____

_____

I am curious about these behaviors: _____

_____

_____

Moving Toward Your Purpose

Exploring your sense of connection to yourself and others holds a lot of power and will be impera-
tive as you work through healing your own trauma and symptoms of PTSD. Connection has the
ability to breathe life back into our soul and makes it possible for us to not just survive but to thrive
through any circumstance.

You were created with purpose and pure intention. One of your greatest tasks during this work
will be learning, or relearning, what you feel your intended purpose in life is. The circumstances you
have been through or endured do not have to define you and often are pivotal in magnifying
passion and purpose when healing occurs. Pain and devastation have the power to strengthen you
and take you to higher levels if you can learn how to stay connected and be present with yourself
along the journey.

Be encouraged; your own truth and vitality still exist within you, waiting to be rediscovered. As you continue on this healing journey with me, you will find your inner truth, self-love, and purpose that you so desire.

The Power of Imagination

Imagination and storytelling can be found throughout history and across cultures. Storytelling has been shown to influence, teach, and inspire hope and unity, and requires our imaginative processes. Just as survival is hardwired in our brain, so is imagination. The power of imagination has been shown to inspire healing and will be used throughout your work in this book. Here is an example of how the power of imagination can instill life, hope, and healing.

Jordan grew up in a chronically unsafe family environment. Both of her parents were abusive and struggled with substance abuse and mental health problems. Throughout the years of turmoil in her household, she and her younger brother were exposed to physical, emotional, and psychological abuse along with ongoing periods of neglect. When her parents were high on substances or away from home for days on end, she would make daily journeys to the local food bank to ensure that she and her brother could eat. Eventually, she and her brother were removed from the home by the state.

When Jordan arrived for her first counseling session, she was in her mid-twenties and married with four children. She reported experiencing anxiety attacks, nightmares, flashbacks, panic, and an all-encompassing, paralyzing fear that had limited her ability to work and function on a daily basis. After a thorough assessment, I diagnosed Jordan with PTSD as a result of her early trauma. I knew that beginning to teach her a coping technique would be helpful in her day-to-day life. I educated her on EMDR and introduced her to an exercise entitled "Calm Place." I explained that I was going to have her imagine a place that represented a sense of calm and peacefulness. She was quick to doubt her ability to envision such a calm place. She explained that she could not remember ever feeling a true sense of calm in her lifetime. I encouraged her to see what came to mind, and she reluctantly allowed me to guide her through the exercise.

Jordan explained that she envisioned herself sitting up on a hill looking down on her local church building. She went on to describe a beautiful, lush field of flowers in vibrant colors and a wide-open blue sky. As Jordan looked down upon the town, she recalled seeing her husband and their children contentedly playing in the field of flowers. She said she just watched them playing in this place. Tears started slowly dripping down her face, and when she finally found the words to continue, she explained that she hadn't felt so peaceful in years. Surprised by what came to her mind, Jordan stated that her tears represented gratitude and relief from being able to experience such peacefulness. As we continued with the exercise, I prompted her to select a mantra or belief that she would like to hold about the place she chose, and she came up with the statement "I am safe now."

In a later session, Jordan shared that she would frequently use this exercise on her own when she wanted to feel safe or grounded. She would recall and slowly allow herself to relax and acknowledge her deep feeling state of being calm and present in the moment.

In therapy, we would frequently return to Jordan's calm place after processing some of her most painful traumas associated with her PTSD. Each time, she would be able to see herself with her loved ones, free of the plagues of abuse she had once endured. During a session involving a memory from childhood, she imagined going back in time, taking her child self by the hand, leading her out of her abusive home and into her calm place. She pictured her current self kneeling down and telling her child self that she could stay in this calm place and finally be a kid. She imagined being safe, free from abuse, and playing in the field of flowers with her own children and husband.

Jordan couldn't explain the feeling of relief she experienced imagining her child self in a safe place. She eventually had the image of her calm place painted and hung in her home as a reminder that beauty, peace, and safety can still be found, if even just in the horizon of our imagination.

I want to guide you through your own Calm Place exercise. This exercise was developed by the creator of EMDR, Francine Shapiro (Shapiro 2018). However, before we begin, I would like to introduce you to an added form of stimulation that we will use during some of the activities throughout the rest of this book. It is the same method that I use with all my clients and that I used with Jordan. In the next chapter, I will go further into detail about why I recommend these additive forms of stimulation and how they apply to EMDR.

For now, we will stick with one method in particular, called the "butterfly hug." We will use this in the Calm Place activity to follow.

Butterfly Hug

To begin, cross your arms across your chest, as if you are giving yourself a hug, with each hand resting on your shoulder or arm of the opposite side of your body. As you keep your arms crossed across your chest, slowly begin by tapping your hands on your shoulders or arms, alternating taps from right to left at a rate and pressure that is comfortable but noticeable. Imagine the cadence of a pendulum as you tap from right to left. Continue tapping from side to side for about one minute, just focusing on your breath and being present, aware of your current physical sensations and staying in the moment.

Now, let's combine the butterfly hug with the Calm Place exercise for our first EMDR activity.

Calm Place

Calm Place is an activity that will help you learn ways to manage symptoms and triggers related to your trauma or symptoms of PTSD. It is a "change state" exercise (Shapiro 2018). This means that you can learn to change your own feelings, regulate your emotions, and create a place that is calm and peaceful in the inner workings of your mind. I have recorded an audio version of this exercise to ease you through this and help you get comfortable with the process. You can download this and additional exercises from http://www.newharbinger.com/49586. It might be easier for you to listen to the steps rather than read them. Choose whatever works best for you.

To begin, identify a place that is calming and relaxing. It can be a place that you have or haven't visited or one that is completely imagined. Try and pick a place that represents peace, tranquility, and joy. This place can be used in meditation and grounding exercises or for calming and relaxation purposes. (You can download and listen to audio recordings of a guided meditation and guided deep breathing at http://www.newharbinger.com/49586.) We will refer back to this exercise throughout our work together, just as I did with Jordan.

Pick a place or image that feels calm and safe to you. It may be helpful for you to read through this exercise a few times until you are familiar with the steps and can do it easily from memory.

To begin:

1. Find a comfortable, quiet place and position. I will let you know when to add the butterfly hug and when to stop using it. When I prompt you to use the butterfly hug, you will do it for approximately 30–60 seconds.

2. Next, I would like you to use the butterfly hug that you learned above. Remember to do this at a rate and pressure that is comfortable for you.

3. As you continue with the butterfly hug tapping, go ahead and close your eyes and take a moment to just be present with yourself. Notice your particular thoughts, feelings, emotions,

and sensations within your body. Just listen and observe as you tune in to your inner world. After about 30 seconds, open your eyes and stop the butterfly hug tapping. What did you notice going on in your inner world?

_____

_____

_____

_____

4. Now, begin the butterfly hug and tapping as you continue to focus on the image of the place that you have in mind. Continue to tap and think of each of the following as you tap (it may be helpful to make notes to help you connect with the sensations of this place in the future):

Sight: Notice everything that you see in this place—the colors, time of day, sights, and if anyone is with you or if you are alone.

_____

_____

_____

_____

Smell: Notice what you smell in this place.

_____

_____

_____

_____

Hearing: Listen to all the sounds in this place; are they quiet, soft, loud, soothing? Is there music or talking?

_____

_____

_____

_____

Taste: Notice if you are eating or drinking anything in this place.

_____

_____

_____

_____

Touch/Physical: Notice what you are doing in this place. Are you sitting, standing, being still or active? Notice how you feel physically in this place. Notice the temperature of this place, if it is warm or cool. Notice how you feel emotionally in this place.

_____

_____

_____

_____

5. After you have thought of each of the sensations of your calm place, take a deep breath in and out and stop your butterfly hug. Take a moment to identify anything that came up and write about what you noticed.

_____

_____

_____

_____

Now, identify a positive statement, or mantra, that resonates with you and would remind you of this place that came to mind and the feelings it evoked. For example, this could be "I am strong" or "I can have peace" or "I am okay." Note whatever comes to mind that represents the feeling of this place: _____.

6. Close your eyes, taking a deep breath in and out as you begin your butterfly hug again. Bring up your calm place in your mind and notice all of the sensations: the smells, sounds, sights, physical feelings, emotions, and anything else that comes up. As you notice these sensations, think of your positive statement or mantra and continue with your butterfly hug. After about 30–60 seconds, you can stop. What did you notice? What specific imagery or sensations stood out to you?

    _____

    _____

    _____

    _____

7. Taking a deep breath in and out, begin your butterfly hug and continue with it as you bring up your calm place once more. Now, imagine that you could take the calm of this place and spread this feeling throughout your entire body until you feel completely at peace and your body feels fully relaxed. Do this for about 30–60 seconds, and when you feel completely relaxed, stop your butterfly hug and open your eyes. What thoughts, feelings, sensations, or images stood out the most to you?

    _____

    _____

    _____

    _____

    _____

Take a moment and reflect on any discoveries or realizations that you had from completing the Calm Place exercise. How will this exercise be useful to you and what hope does it inspire?

_____

_____

_____

_____

_____

I recommend that you practice this exercise in the morning, before bed, or anytime you feel distressed and have a need to calm down or regroup your emotions. As you work on healing from distressing past traumatic events, it will offer you a place of retreat to calm your brain and body down, give you temporary relief from your trauma processing, and help you to better cope with the lingering effects of PTSD.

You can return to this exercise anytime you would like to or need to when feeling emotional, tense, or highly stressed. We will also return to this exercise at times during our work together, so it may be helpful to practice it on your own several times to familiarize yourself with it.

Identify Your Promises of Change

Take a moment and select the top three promises, or goals, you hope to achieve by learning and practicing EMDR. Rate these in order of importance from 1 to 3, with 1 being the most important for you.

☐ I am beginning to find relief from painful past experiences.

☐ I will experience a new sense of emotional freedom, happiness, or peace.

☐ I will no longer regret or be fearful of the past.

☐ I will embrace the notion that my experience and story matter and can be used to help others.

☐ I will have more self-confidence and a sense of purpose and meaning in my life.

☐ I will have a change of attitude and more positive outlook on my life.

☐ My fear of others, myself, and the world will begin to leave me.

☐ I will know how to face difficult situations and will embrace these situations in spite of fear.

☐ I will begin to see myself in a loving, compassionate manner.

It may be helpful for you to come back to this list of promises or goals that you hope to achieve as a way of seeing the progress that you are experiencing.

The Hero's Journey

I believe that there is a hero in each of us. In each of your own stories, you are likely the true hero. Just as Jordan became the hero in her story and led her past traumatized self to freedom and safety, you will discover that there is a hero within you as well. To become a hero over the trials in your life, a few things are required:

- First, you must learn something from the darkness you have faced that you have come to recognize today as a strength.

- Second, you must identify the value of all experiences, whether positive or negative.

- Third, you must be willing to face your fears, vulnerability, pain, and most of all yourself.

- And lastly, you must recognize your potential and restore your own hope.

Try and answer some of these questions:

1. What strengths have you acquired as a result of the trials you have faced?

   _____

   _____

   _____

2. What have you come to value in your life due to these past difficult experiences?

   _____

   _____

   _____

3. What are the fears and inner barriers that still get in your way?

_____

_____

_____

4. What potential do you know exists within you?

_____

_____

_____

5. What do you want your narrative of yourself to be at the end of your life?

_____

_____

_____

Some of these questions may seem difficult or impossible to answer right now, and that is okay; you don't have to have the answers right now. You are going to find them. You may be wondering how I can be so certain. The answer is simple: you are here now, reading this, bettering yourself and searching for meaning and freedom. Only true heroes do that.

CHAPTER TWO

Learn Your Essential Tools

When we are tired we will fight the wrong battles.

—Steven Furtick

Every experience you have had so far in your life is a stepping-stone. Together, these form bits and pieces of your own learning path, giving you tools to prepare you as you move toward living your best life. This may be a hard concept to grasp or believe when pain has followed you, or even haunted you. However, this outlook can be essential to reclaiming your power and tapping into your own healing. When we become consumed by the grief and heartache, we ultimately surrender our power and can lose our way.

By learning skills such as bilateral stimulation techniques, working to redefine your ideal self, and developing your own team of allies, you will begin to reclaim your strength. I know that you want to do whatever it takes to overcome your hurt. I know that you desire to believe in yourself again…or for the first time. This is where you get to start recreating yourself as the hero of your own story. Learning and practicing the essential skills and tools of EMDR contained in this chapter will no doubt begin to propel you forward on your path of healing.

Why EMDR Is Effective at Treating Trauma and PTSD

Before learning these essential tools for EMDR, it's important to have a solid understanding of how and why EMDR (eye movement desensitization and reprocessing) works. EMDR, like many trauma-informed approaches, is based on the framework that your body and mind are strongly connected. When painful things happen to us, these experiences can get saved in ways that cause glitches (in the form of flashbacks, emotions, behaviors, and memories) in our brain. This happens because the experiences didn't make it to the correct storage part of the brain (van der Kolk 2014). EMDR helps bad or painful memories get unstuck and moved to more functional parts of the brain. It does this by activating the *adaptive information processing system*, the brain's natural healing system, which we discussed in the previous chapter. Just as you learned about the REM cycle, this system is activated by using *bilateral stimulation*, stimulation that activates the right and left hemispheres of the brain, such as the butterfly hug you learned in chapter one. This bilateral stimulation allows your brain to be fully online while also engaging the body with external stimulus through the tapping. By engaging both the emotional and logical portions of the brain, this process helps to desensitize you to triggers and discover new insights and perspectives. The goal of EMDR is to take the power out of your past experiences, tap into your own natural healing process, and assist you in seeing yourself in a new positive way so that you are no longer stuck.

Consider what your personal goals are for learning EMDR. What symptoms are you hoping to relieve?

_____

_____

_____

_____

Remember from chapter one that the brain operates like a stoplight and is merely trying to help ensure survival. Part of what makes EMDR so effective is that it helps your brain access the "stuck" parts of the trauma you have faced (like the sensory reactions and responses you learned about earlier). In fact, it is so effective at reducing symptoms that most people report having a large reduction in their emotional and physical reactions to triggers after just a few sessions (Shapiro 2018).

Over the past few decades, researchers have come to understand that trauma (an event or experience that negatively changes the way we see ourselves, others, and the world around us) requires a different treatment approach than talk therapy or other traditional forms of psychotherapy. EMDR does not require talking in detail about difficult experiences. It does not focus solely on your emotions, thoughts, or behaviors, but rather assists your brain in engaging in its natural healing. Much of talk therapy requires the front part of the brain, your green light region, to be engaged and online. However, as we learned in chapter one, when trauma is triggered, this frontal region of the brain is offline and we are functioning from a red light—fight, flight, or freeze—response. This is why it is often difficult to apply reason and make sound decisions in regard to trauma because in order to do so, your ability to use logic and reasoning must be intact.

In order for the green light region of your brain (which allows you to problem solve, brainstorm, and use logic) to be fully online and operational when processing this stuck trauma, your brain and body need "dual attention." Dual attention, or dual awareness, simply means that we are activating and keeping both the yellow light region and the logical green light region of your brain engaged. This is done with a variety of methods, all of which involve bilateral stimulation—stimulating the right side of the body and then the left.

Research in EMDR has shown that this method, when used while working through trauma and PTSD, helps keep your brain online. This way, it can utilize all its parts required for optimal functioning to get rid of the stuck symptoms that you continue to wrestle with. Let's look at how EMDR can be instrumental in assisting the mind.

The Power to Heal Intrusive Thoughts

As you have been walking through life carrying your own pain and baggage, you have surely run into certain thoughts or memories, big or small, that seem to seep into your mind. These intrusions likely leave you feeling stuck or spiraling in a flood of emotions, unable to escape. For example, it could be loud sounds, such as fireworks, that send you into a spiral. It could be seeing unknown messages on your partner's phone, or a specific smell. When these reminders pop up, you may avoid going to certain celebrations where loud noises occur, or you may isolate yourself and avoid certain festivities and social events. You may be lost in confusion about why these recurring elements continue to disturb your life and prevent you from doing the things you most desire, rob you of joy and peace, and leave a flood of hopelessness in their aftermath. I want to share an example with you to further illustrate what these barriers can look like in your life, what the goal of EMDR is, and how it relates to helping you work through your own personal barriers.

> Maria was in her sixties when I began seeing her. She was raised by a single mom who suffered from severe, untreated obsessive-compulsive disorder (OCD). Most of her childhood was plagued by her mother's bizarre, compulsive rituals, emotional abuse, and abandonment. When she came home from school, she was never allowed to come in through the front door and instead had to enter through the garage. Upon entering the garage, she would be required to completely undress on an arrangement of newspapers that her mother had carefully laid out. Her mother would then scrub Maria down with a brush and carry her to the bathroom to ensure that she did not "contaminate" the home. She would have to sit in the bathtub, unable to touch anything, including the sides of the tub. Afterward, she had to go to the basement, where she remained for the rest of the evening. This series of events was repeated daily.
>
> Maria explained that in the summers when school was not in session, she would be kept in the garage all day while her mother was at work. She was given a paint can to urinate in. Maria told me that she spent most of her days using her imagination to survive the loneliness and despair.

The hauntings of these childhood memories still seemed to follow her, at times relentlessly, reappearing in the forefront of her mind. When triggered with these thoughts, a doorway would open to all of her past trauma, anger, resentment, mistrust, and fear. Though she could identify all of this as being caused by her mother, when these feelings and emotions resurfaced, they felt real and current. She would be angry, feel abandoned and lied to, as if she could trust no one. Her PTSD symptoms seemed to quickly resume, and she was desperate for answers.

I introduced her to EMDR. Within the first session, her pain was evident as she sifted through memories, past core beliefs that she still held today, and paralyzing fear. Yet she was able to process these in a more definitive way; for the first time, she could describe seeing her pain with both emotion and logic. I watched her slowly begin to find her own answers and realize that she was not as broken as she had thought all along. She concluded that she was not crazy and could in fact learn to trust others despite the hurt that she had endured from her mother in her earlier years. Each session, she made more and more progress and her confidence grew.

After about ten sessions, Maria was completely symptom-free. The pains of her past did not hold the same weight, and she had even come to develop empathy and forgiveness for her mother. During one of our last sessions, she imagined herself tearing down the garage she was once kept in and planting a beautiful garden. She told me how this image gave her relief and freedom from the cell of pain the garage had once represented. She felt free for the first time in her life. She was not emotionally charged around things from her past that once had held so much gravity. Even now, over a year after completing EMDR treatment, she still reports being symptom free.

Your story is unique, just like Maria's. Remember, no matter how big or small, trauma and PTSD affect us all differently. The severity of her PTSD is important, but what's most significant is how it had impacted her brain's ability to cope. It shaped her beliefs around herself, her life, and the way in which she interacted with the world. Some of the most helpful tools that Maria used were envisioning her ideal self and getting to know her restoration team, which you will learn in this chapter. These tools are the gateway that will help you face the once stuck parts of your life that have undermined your functioning. They will allow you to breathe, to be present, and to believe in the positive parts of life again. And most importantly, they will prepare you to heal and teach you to embrace all the parts of your life, good and bad.

As you begin utilizing these EMDR tools, you will discover that *you* have all your own answers—you have all the knowledge and insight necessary to break free from your past. You will find that your therapist is merely a guide and that *you* are the master of your inner world. The answers you will discover and the empowerment you will uncover will be life-changing. As you learn to lean on your own understanding, you will find that the self-doubt you have struggled with for so long will begin to lessen and your confidence and belief in yourself will expand. Your mind is a beautiful place full of learning, capability, creativity, and forgiveness.

The first, and critical, step in learning EMDR tools and techniques is to learn bilateral stimulation. When both sides of the nervous system are awakened by stimulating each side of the body, your brain begins firing neurons in both your right and left hemispheres, which is essential for optimal brain functions such as concentration, problem solving, and emotion regulation. Let's learn some of the different variations of bilateral stimulation together.

Bilateral Stimulation Techniques

I will describe four bilateral stimulation methods, including the butterfly hug, all of which are ways to achieve dual awareness. Feel free to practice and try out a few of the different options listed here. You may find one in particular that works best for you, and this may be the method you choose to use moving forward in our work together (Shapiro 2018).

Eye movements. Begin by raising two fingers from the same hand in front of your line of sight, and move them from right to left, with your eyes tracking them as you move your fingers back and forth. Find a speed that you are able to comfortably track and a distance that feels easy to focus on. If holding up your fingers is not comfortable, you can also try moving your eyes from one corner of the room in front of you to the other corner of the room, and slowly shifting your vision from corner to corner at a speed that is comfortable and makes it easy to focus. In the Resources list located on the website for this book (http://www.newharbinger.com/49586), I have provided a few apps that offer visual aids to assist with the eye movements, should you choose this as your method of bilateral stimulation.

Butterfly hug. Begin by crossing your arms across your chest, as if you are giving yourself a hug. As you leave your arms across your chest, with your hands resting lightly on your shoulders or upper arms, start tapping your hands from right to left. Alternate between tapping the right, then the left, continuously. Use a rate and pressure that is comfortable but noticeable.

Knee tapping. In a sitting position, lay your hands on the tops of your knees and tap lightly from right to left, continually, at a rate and pressure that is comfortable but noticeable.

Auditory stimulation. This form of bilateral stimulation involves listening to sounds in one ear and then the other, alternating sound from right to left ears throughout the exercise. In the Resources list (see http://www.newharbinger.com/49586), there are several resources and apps that provide information for sounds that you can download. This will work best if you use headphones and ensure that the sound plays from just the right speaker of your headphones and then just the left. This enhances the bilateral stimulation so that it occurs more efficiently in your nervous system.

When doing the exercises in this book, choose whichever bilateral stimulation method works best for you and makes you feel comfortable. For now, just know that this process is helping your brain to stay "awake" and "alert" and will assist you with processing and healing some of your own wounds.

Identify Your Ideal Self

Now that you've learned four options for bilateral stimulation, it's time to put EMDR to practice. I want to introduce you to a useful exercise that will help strengthen your self-worth and emotional resiliency and help you feel less alone. This exercise was adapted from Francine Shapiro and Laurel Parnell's work of resourcing (Shapiro 2018; Parnell 2018). Using EMDR and imagery, this exercise will help you recognize the strengths, capabilities, and resources that you hold inside yourself. I will be referencing this exercise frequently throughout your EMDR journey, and you can practice it whenever you feel it necessary. An audio version of this exercise is available for download at http://www.newharbinger.com/49586.

If you're not using the audio recording, it may be helpful for you to read through this exercise a few times until you are familiar with the steps and can do it easily from memory. It may also be helpful to make notes as you read through it the first time. This can help you connect with the sensations and imagery of this exercise.

Finally, please review the four types of bilateral stimulation techniques described above and choose the type you will be using for this exercise, listed here in shortened form.

Eye movements. Move two fingers (on the same hand) back and forth from right to left, tracking them with your eyes, at a comfortable speed and distance. Alternatively, you can move your eyes back and forth from one corner of the room to the other.

Butterfly hug. Cross your arms across your chest, as if giving yourself a hug. Rest your hands lightly on your shoulders or upper arms, and alternate tapping your hands from right to left continuously. Use a rate and pressure that is comfortable but noticeable.

Knee tapping. In a sitting position, lay your hands on the tops of your knees and tap lightly from right to left, continually, at a rate and pressure that is comfortable but noticeable.

Auditory stimulation. Select a sound to download from the Resources list available on the website for this book (http://www.newharbinger.com/49586). Using headphones, ensure that the sound plays from just the right speaker of your headphones and then just the left speaker of your headphones.

Choose whichever bilateral stimulation method works for you and makes you feel comfortable. I will tell you when to add the bilateral stimulation and when to stop using it. When I prompt you to use the bilateral stimulation, you will do it for approximately 30–60 seconds.

To begin:

1. Find a comfortable, quiet place and position.

2. Now, take a moment and imagine yourself at your best. This can be an image of yourself in the future achieving goals you have set or a time that you felt the happiest or most secure. Pick an image of you that makes you feel hopeful. Describe yourself and what you are doing here:

    _____

    _____

    _____

3. Once you have a positive image of yourself in mind, close your eyes, take a deep breath in and out, and begin your method of bilateral stimulation. Continue with this as you focus on the image of your ideal, best self. After about 30 seconds, stop your bilateral stimulation and notice whatever feelings arise or whatever came to mind.

    _____

    _____

    _____

4. Take another breath in and out, and consider as many details as possible about yourself as you envision this image of you at your best. Then begin your method of bilateral stimulation. Consider these details regarding your ideal self:

    •   Where would you be? _____

    •   How old would you be? _____

    •   Notice what you would be doing with your time. _____

    •   What would your personal life look life? _____

    •   What would your hobbies and interests be? _____

5. Take a deep breath in and out and stop your bilateral stimulation. You may take a moment and jot down any answers that came to mind from the questions above. Also notice how your body and mind are feeling.

6. Begin your bilateral stimulation again as you imagine your ideal self. This time as you do, consider the following:

   - How would you feel about yourself? _____

   - How would you handle your feelings and emotions? _____

   - How would you resolve conflict? _____

   - How would you engage and interact with others in your life? _____

7. After considering these prompts, go ahead and stop your bilateral stimulation, taking several deep breaths in and out. Write down whatever came to mind.

8. Beginning your bilateral stimulation once more, notice the confidence and strength you would carry as your ideal self. As you do your bilateral stimulation and hold this image in your mind, notice:

   - Is there is anything that your ideal self would encourage you to do in your own life, right now?

   _____

   - Is there something that your ideal self would want to remind you of? Perhaps your own strength or courage?

   _____

9. Take a deep breath in and out and stop your bilateral stimulation. Take a moment to write down all you noticed or thought of.

10. Close your eyes once more and resume your bilateral stimulation, bringing up the image of your ideal self once more. Just notice what your ideal self wants you to recognize within

yourself that is positive. When you have a strong sense of feeling positive, or strong, you can open your eyes and stop your bilateral stimulation. Note what came to mind.

_____

_____

_____

Take a moment to reflect on any discoveries or realizations you had from completing this exercise and seeing yourself at your best. How will this exercise be useful to you and what hope does it inspire?

_____

_____

_____

_____

_____

I hope you recognize that you already hold many of the traits that you identified within your ideal self. You are capable of growing and learning to become all you are meant to be.

Identify Your Triggers

We all react to things in unwanted ways, based on our past experiences. For example, let's say that you were subjected to the physical and emotional torture of witnessing a fellow police officer lose their life to gunfire on a pursuit of a dangerous suspect. In order to survive and exist during this chaotic time, your brain did not have time to problem solve or rationally think through this occurrence. Instead, it was hardwired to react and respond in order to protect you from any threatened or potential violence. Now, years later, you may find yourself struggling to problem solve or think through emotions when you are triggered by the geographical location of this past event. You may even have the innate response to react by fighting or by avoiding conflict at all costs. This is how your brain operates and ensures survival: rather than selecting what is most effective in the moment, it uses what it knows and has experienced. In essence, your brain

- gets rid of things it doesn't use;

- naturally holds on to, and continues to function strictly with, the parts that it is accustomed to habitually using; and

- uses coping skills, responses, and behaviors based on what is familiar and most readily available.

In order to learn how to handle ongoing distress, and life in general, we'll first identify your triggers—the types of people, places, or situations that lead you to react in negative, unwanted ways. This is an important step in learning to become desensitized to these triggers to lessen their effect in your life.

In chapter one, we explored how your brain responds to sensory details, and you identified the senses that you tend to notice the most. Now, I want you to take this a step further and elaborate on the particular sensory details that trigger you to respond in unhelpful ways.

Take a moment and list as many triggers and responses as you can identify for each of the following categories. For example, for sight, any time I see the first name of my past abuser, I am instantly triggered and anxious. And for smell, any time I smell popcorn, I am instantly reminded of being assaulted outside a movie theater and become paralyzed or angry. Feel free to come back and add to this list any time you recall a trigger. Bringing awareness to our triggers usually takes time, so be patient with yourself and this process, but also be as thorough as possible.

Sight: What objects, people, places, words, or images are triggering for you; cause you to feel anxious, agitated, or frozen; or lead to your wanting to avoid or escape?

_____

_____

_____

What is your basic response when you experience the above identified triggers (e.g., anxiety, feeling paralyzed, anger, the urge to isolate)?

_____

_____

Smell: What smells cause you to have disturbing memories; result in your feeling anxious, agitated, or frozen; or lead to your wanting to avoid or escape?

_____

_____

_____

What is your basic response when you experience the above identified triggers (e.g., anxiety, feeling paralyzed, anger, the urge to isolate)?

_____

_____

Taste: What tastes lead you to having unwanted memories; result in your feeling anxious, agitated, or frozen; or lead to your wanting to avoid or escape?

_____

_____

_____

What is your basic response when you experience the above identified triggers?

_____

_____

Touch: What physical sensations (e.g., textures, places on your body being touched) lead you to having unwanted memories; result in you feeling anxious, agitated, or frozen; or lead to your wanting to avoid or escape?

_____

_____

_____

What is your basic response when you experience the above identified triggers?

_____

_____

Sound: What sounds (e.g., songs, loud noises) lead you to having unwanted memories; result in your feeling anxious, agitated, or frozen; or lead to your wanting to avoid or escape?

_____

_____

_____

What is your basic response when you experience the above identified triggers?

_____

_____

I hope you will not judge yourself for the responses you listed. You are exploring these triggers and reactions to build awareness and assist you as you identify ways to target and lessen these responses.

There can be different trigger responses depending on the type and degree of threat we feel. For myself, I tend to have a fight response when I feel someone is trying to hurt a loved one. However, when I feel that I am being emotionally rejected or abandoned, I will most often have a freeze response and become unable to speak or stand up for myself; in these cases I tend to daydream or check out. For you, perhaps the fight response can look like actual physical fighting. Or maybe this could look like emotionally fighting by standing your ground and not backing down from an argument. This could also look like retaliation, yelling, conflict with authority, and so on.

In what types of situations or circumstances do you find yourself being triggered with unwanted reactions?

_____

_____

_____

As you learned earlier, trauma has its own memory storage that is separate from your long- and short-term memory. When something dangerous or traumatic occurs, your brain often struggles to filter out these painful life events, and they can become frozen or stuck in time within this trauma memory storage. That is why you have unwanted reactions to the triggers we just explored. Our journey with EMDR will slowly help you access this trauma memory storage and get rid of these stuck memories and symptoms.

Get to Know Your Restoration Team

In the last part of this chapter, I want to leave you with one of the most powerful EMDR exercises. It will help you feel supported when you are faced with fear or feeling alone. This exercise focuses on the support and resources that you have in your life, or your "restoration team." This is an exercise adapted from the work of Laurel Parnell (2018). You can download an audio recording of this exercise at http://www.newharbinger.com/49586.

Begin by identifying people within each of the following roles. Who would fit into each category? Visualize each of these roles and the people in them. What would they say to you, how would they support you, or how would they each remind you? For each category, imagine any figures, dead or alive, real or imagined, fictional characters, animals, or idols that represent that particular role. This could also include your own characteristics that provide that type of support.

You'll notice that "Ideal Self" is the first role listed below; this is because, as we've discussed, within you are many strengths and resources, and you already are—or will become through this work—part of your restoration team.

Ideal Self: Recall the ideal future self that you connected with earlier in this chapter. Imagine yourself as the person you wish to be—yourself at your best.

What would you be doing?

_____

_____

How would you resolve conflict?

_____

_____

How old would you be?

_____

_____

What would you do for work? Enjoyment?

_____

_____

How would you treat others?

_____

_____

How would you treat yourself?

_____

_____

Protectors: These are figures that would keep you safe, watch over you, stand up for you, and be strong when you felt weak. Imagine at least three protectors and notice the type of protection they would provide.

Protector One: _____

_____

_____

Protector Two: _____

_____

_____

Protector Three: _____

_____

_____

Nurturers: These are figures that offer unconditional love, comfort, acceptance, compassion, and nonjudgment. Imagine at least three of these nurturers and write down the nurturing qualities that they would provide.

Nurturer One: _____

_____

_____

Nurturer Two: _____

_____

_____

Nurturer Three: _____

_____

_____

Wise Figures: These are figures that bring sound knowledge, assist you in finding wise answers, offer confidence and certainty, and do not lead you astray. Imagine at least three wise figures and write down the wisdom that they each provide.

Wise Figure One: _____

_____

_____

Wise Figure Two: _____

_____

_____

Wise Figure Three: _____

_____

_____

Spiritual Figures: These are figures that would provide infinite wisdom, faith, and comfort, and remind you that you are being watched over or are connected to something bigger than yourself. Imagine three spiritual figures and write down the comforting guidance that each would provide.

Spiritual Figure One: _____

_____

_____

Spiritual Figure Two: _____

_____

_____

Spiritual Figure Three: _____

_____

_____

Now that you have identified your restoration team, let's add some bilateral stimulation of your choosing. Select the type of bilateral stimulation that you will be using for this exercise: eye movements, butterfly hug, knee tapping, or auditory stimulation. Remember to choose whichever bilateral stimulation method works for you and makes you feel comfortable. I will tell you when to add the bilateral stimulation and when to stop using it. When I prompt you to use the bilateral stimulation, you will do it for approximately 30–60 seconds.

1.   Find a comfortable, quiet place and position.

2.   Close your eyes and take a moment to just be present with yourself. Notice your particular thoughts, feelings, emotions, and even the sensations within your body. Just listen and observe as you tune in to your inner world. After about 30 seconds, open your eyes.

     What did you notice?

     _____

     _____

3.   Breathing in and out, begin your bilateral stimulation. Call to mind each of the figures on your restoration team. Continue with your bilateral stimulation as you imagine:

     •   Your ideal self. Notice the strengths, confidence, joy, and resolve you would have in this ideal state.

     •   Your protectors. Envision their strengths and how they would fight for you, stand up for you, and guard you.

     •   Your nurturing figures. Feel the compassion, love, support, nonjudgment, and loyalty that they provide you.

     •   Your wise figures, with their resolve, confidence, wisdom, support, and guidance.

- Your spiritual figures. Notice their infinite wisdom, the connection they provide, and the faith and healing they would give you.

4. Take a deep breath in and out and stop your bilateral stimulation. What stood out or came to mind during your time of processing?

_____

_____

_____

5. Begin your bilateral stimulation again. Call all these figures to mind and imagine bringing them all together. Imagine what they would do or say to you as you sit here in this moment. Listen to them as they remind you of who you truly are and what you often forget about yourself. What hope would they leave you with? Write down what they have to say, collectively.

_____

_____

_____

6. Embrace their wisdom, love, support, protection, and guidance. Continue with your bilateral stimulation for another 30 seconds.

7. Take a deep breath in and stop your bilateral stimulation.

8. Reflect for a moment and record anything significant, including what they said to you, offered you, or provided you with that you want to bring into your daily life.

_____

_____

_____

_____

9. Allow yourself another deep breath in and out, begin your bilateral stimulation, and once more bring to mind what your restoration team would assure you or remind you of. Is there something that you need to hear from them? Just notice as you continue with this imagery for 30–60 seconds.

10. Take a deep breath in and out and stop your bilateral stimulation. Consider the following questions and write down whatever comes to mind.

- What key messages did your restoration team express?

  _____

  _____

  _____

- What did you need to hear most?

  _____

  _____

  _____

- What, if any, insights or realizations did you find as you listened to your restoration team?

  _____

  _____

  _____

- What would help you see yourself the way in which you envisioned your restoration team seeing you?

  _____

  _____

  _____

This is your personal restoration team. You can utilize this practice anytime you feel that you need additional support or to feel more grounded and connected. Remember that they will be with you on every step of your journey. You do not have to endure this alone. These resources on your restoration team will give you strength, compassion, love, encouragement, wisdom, and grace when you doubt yourself. They are here to remind you that you are enough and that you hold everything inside that you need for the journey that lies ahead.

CHAPTER THREE

Gain Resources for Facing Your Pain

The cave you fear to enter holds the treasure you seek.

—Joseph Campbell

Aisha was a client I saw over the past several years to assist her with her journey of healing due to her husband's continued struggle with substance abuse. Aisha grew up in a supportive, loving home. Shortly after marrying her husband, Greg, she discovered that he had a drug addiction and felt unprepared to cope with the challenge. Nonetheless, she stayed by his side as he battled and faced his addiction for decades. Recovery phases would come and life would feel normal when a relapse would occur and rock the foundation they both had worked so hard to create. However, their marriage, and their love for each other, remained solid. During one particular session, Aisha reported that Greg had just left on a motorcycle ride with dozens of other men in recovery, their son was going to be married in less than a week, and she was back in school to finish her nursing degree—all typical life stressors.

Tragically, the very next day Greg died in a motorcycle accident while with his sober riders crew. Aisha came back in about a week after the funeral and was devastated. She never imagined life without him. She described feeling earth-shattering pain after his loss. In addition, she told me that she was dealing with all the debt and bills that had been hanging over them while Greg was working toward sobriety over the past several years, and she was going to have to file for bankruptcy and sell the home that they had built together. Tears streamed down her face as she described not being able to imagine moving forward without him. She stated that it wasn't just the loss of Greg that was so traumatic, but also the ripple effects: the memories, the holidays, and all the life changes that would transpire without him.

I continued to see her as she learned to navigate this new life that was coated with unfamiliarity and grief. Amid all the pain, loss, and trauma of his death, she agreed to try some

EMDR, specifically the restoration team exercise. As she did, she identified Greg, still ever-present in her mind and heart, as one of her protectors. With tears, she concluded this allowed her to find an inkling of hope that he would always be with her. Her strength and resilience were things I have always been amazed by. Aisha did not know how to give up. In fact, she knew the opposite—she knew how to live.

I had watched her trudge through mountains of uncertainty, heartache, and fear in the past and continued to watch her as the life she knew was stripped from underneath her. Through her sessions of EMDR after Greg's loss, she processed her immense grief, shared the blessings that followed even in the pain, and maintained hope that Greg would still help her get by. Returning to the restoration team exercise frequently, she would draw hope and internal resolve. She envisioned Greg reminding her that she had done many hard things in her life before and that she would somehow find her way back again. This isn't to say that she was able to easily move on or that the pain eventually resolved. The pain remained, all very real and at times even raw, and with whatever came she learned to embrace the emotions, lessons, miracles, and traumatic loss.

I share Aisha's experience because her demonstration of acceptance and reframing her trauma, along with her resilience, is something that I hope can inspire you as you rewrite your own painful experiences.

The start of your journey will require you to face your pain. I know this can feel terrifying and overwhelming; that's why I'm devoting a full chapter to this topic. You may be wondering why it is even necessary to face your pain. Or wondering if it will cause more setbacks than freedom to examine these hurts. All of these fears are understandable. We are used to numbing out, avoiding, or coping with the pain in a variety of ways already, maybe with drinking, eating, daydreaming, sleeping, or overworking. Avoiding our pain is merely our own survival instincts trying to protect us in circumstances where we have learned or had no other options but to simply stay afloat. But the more we avoid the pain, the more we still suffer inside. The pain lies dormant right under the surface. We could continue to cope, numb out, and avoid, but if this is what we choose, nothing will change. The pain will still be there and we will remain stuck where we are. If we don't work through it, we will feel it anyway.

Remember that as scary as change, vulnerability, and tackling your pain may feel, you have other choices now besides sheer survival. Learning to turn toward your feelings and emotions is a stepping-stone that will assist you in breaking the chains you carry. Acknowledge that up until this point, you have done what you can in order to endure things beyond your own comprehension or control. Honor that these past survival skills served a purpose, but just like training wheels on a bike, there comes a time when they are no longer needed. That time is now. When you allow this to occur, you will find that it is possible to face your fears, emotions, and experiences with self-compassion. You will learn ways to forgive yourself for where you were lacking, coping, or merely surviving and you will begin to grow, heal, and ultimately embrace life and yourself.

Finding Trust and Connection Within Yourself

A large part of your healing work and understanding of your own experiences will require reestablishing trust within yourself. Trust is difficult to develop after we have experienced any level of trauma. We quickly learn that the unexpected could occur at any time and, as a result, we may have a tendency to be constantly on guard. But trust is where healing starts as we learn to develop compassionate curiosity for our experiences of trauma.

Take a moment to reflect. What does it feel like to be encouraged to trust yourself?

_____

_____

_____

What has kept you from trusting yourself until now?

_____

_____

_____

What do you feel would help you learn to trust in yourself? Do you need encouragement? Understanding? Compassion from someone who knows what you've been through? You can offer yourself these things and more. Write down what you need.

_____

_____

_____

Focusing on what you need will help you to gain confidence as you move forward. Identifying these needs will give you security and faith in the future when you are faced with pain, heartache, and other deep emotions and experiences.

Building Self-Compassion

To be able to face yourself and whatever pain you hold, and to trust that you are your best supporter, it's crucial to grasp the concept of compassion. Understanding and choosing to commit to practicing self-compassion is essential for your path of healing. In fact, compassion is so essential to instigating change that it can been seen in pivotal social changes throughout history. Change requires compassion. Since you are on your own walk of personal change, I hope this resonates. Self-compassion is likely something that you desperately crave.

So what is compassion? The Latin origin of compassion means "to suffer with." Breathe this thought in. The promise that this original meaning conveys is what makes it so powerful. It ultimately conveys that suffering is not a solo act.

Buddhists have used compassion for centuries in their practices and have expanded the meaning of compassion to encapsulate "loving-kindness" and "friendship." They describe compassion as an action that includes being mindful of their thoughts and feelings, noticing their internal motivations, and cultivating awareness for themselves and others.

Consider compassion as an action or practice rather than simply an emotion. Compassion is simply acknowledging your emotions and experiencing your feelings. It sometimes helps to envision your emotions or feelings as a visitor who is passing through. The visitors of pain and other feelings you encounter are there to be noticed and felt and to assist you in learning new lessons and healing old wounds.

Compassion is the ability to see others and yourself with value, respect, and empathy. It allows you to see past your pain and mistakes to your true worth and purpose. Brené Brown (2010), renowned author, describes compassion in this way:

> When we practice generating compassion, we can expect to experience our fear of pain. Compassion is daring. It involves learning to relax and allow ourselves to move gently towards what scares us… [I]n cultivating compassion we draw from the wholeness of our experience—our suffering, our empathy, as well as our cruelty and terror. It has to be this way.

I want to help you face your pain with compassion. Consider what self-compassion looks like to you. I encourage you to find a photo that represents a time when you felt a strong sense of kindness and compassion toward yourself. If you do not have a specific picture, feel free to use magazines, other images, words, quotes, or even draw symbols that would convey feelings of self-compassion.

Draw, paste, or write your images or symbol of self-compassion here.

Self-compassion can often assist you in revealing your personal strengths. Write down three inner strengths you have.

1. _____

2. _____

3. _____

How might self-compassion help you heal your trauma or PTSD?

_____

_____

_____

_____

_____

As you explore your trauma or PTSD, I'll continue to teach you how to face your pain in a more gracious way—a way that will allow you to discover the resiliency and strength that lie within, and beyond, your pain.

Your Resiliency Time Line

This exercise, developed by Regina D. Morrow, will help you identify your past and current strengths, influential and supportive people you have encountered, and positive experiences you have had throughout your life. Identifying these positive resources will assist you in offering yourself compassionate support as you face your pain.

On the time line that follows, I invite you to record those experiences or people that have been the most significant or impactful to you. The time line is written in five-year increments; however, it can be modified as needed should you need more room.

Next to each age block on the time line, list the events, people, or accomplishments using just a simple description, name, or a few short words. Examples include recognitions, awards, promotions, special opportunities, births, marriages, celebrations, holidays, learning a new skill, graduating, trips, pets, meaningful friendships, mentors, teachers, family members who were loving and supportive, career goals, reuniting with others, and conquering a fear.

Write events from age 0 to 50 to the left of the line. Write events from age 50 to 100 to the right of the line. Feel free to use different colors or symbols or any other methods you choose to help you depict the entries. You can come back to this as needed and add to the time line as you recall more. Now, go ahead and fill in your resiliency time line.

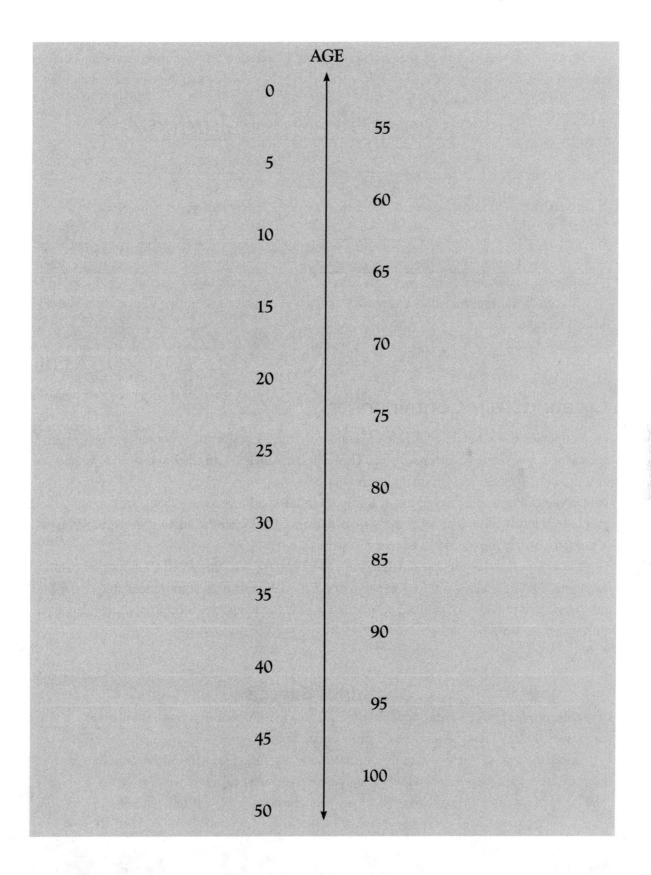

Take a moment to reflect on the resources, strengths, abilities, positive experiences, and influential people that you listed in your time line. How have they assisted you in getting through some of the challenges and trauma you have faced?

_____

_____

_____

_____

_____

Hold on to this resiliency time line and use it as a way to begin recognizing your strengths, abilities, and resiliencies.

Creating Your Container

I want to teach you a skill that will help you cope with triggers or startling emotions you may experience as you move forward with your work. The skill that I am going to teach you is what we refer to as a grounding technique. Grounding techniques, such as guided meditation and deep breathing (which you can find audio recordings of at http://www.newharbinger.com/49586), are coping strategies that help you shift your focus away from negative experiences to more positive thoughts or sensations by drawing your focus to your five senses.

You can utilize this exercise anytime you experience triggers, unwanted memories, or painful emotions. The skill allows you to distance yourself from disturbances, annoyances, and/or day-to-day stressors. It provides a container, or space, that will offer temporary relief from these disruptive, unresolved stressors.

Container Exercise

It may be helpful for you to read through this exercise a few times until you are familiar with it. You can also download an audio recording of the exercise at http://www.newharbinger.com/49586.

Select the type of bilateral stimulation that you will be using for this exercise: eye movements, butterfly hug, knee tapping, or auditory stimulation. Remember to choose whichever bilateral stimulation method works for you and makes you feel comfortable. I will tell you when to add the bilateral stimulation and when to stop using it. When I prompt you to use the bilateral stimulation, you will do it for approximately 30–60 seconds.

Remember that adding the bilateral stimulation will assist you in connecting more fully to your imagined experience as well as keeping you present, in the here and now.

To begin:

1. Find a comfortable, quiet place and position.

2. Imagine an object that is secure, strong, and able to hold things. This object will be something you can easily put things into but not easily get things out of (e.g., it may need a lock, key, or combination to open), such as a safe, a chest, and a lockbox. Please describe your container here:

   _____

3. Once you have an object in mind, close your eyes, take a deep breath in and out, and begin your bilateral stimulation while you envision your container or object. Continuing with your bilateral stimulation, consider the following:

   • **Sight:** Notice everything that you can about this object (e.g., the size, texture, location, color, other details).

   • **Smell:** Notice if this object has a certain smell.

   • **Sound:** Imagine that this object is soundproof, and notice how sound cannot leave this object.

   • **Touch/Physical:** Imagine how this object feels, what it is made of, and how it would be opened and closed. Notice how it would stay secure or locked.

4. After you have thought of each of the sensations of your container, take a deep breath in and out and stop your bilateral stimulation. Describe the specific details of your container below:

   Sight: _____

   Smell: _____

   Sound: _____

   Physical touch: _____

5. Now, take another deep breath in and out, and begin your bilateral stimulation as you bring to mind a specific disturbance—for instance, a thought, worry, fear, or episode of anger—you have had recently. Pay attention to what specifically comes to mind as you reflect on this. Continue with this visualization for approximately 30 seconds, and then stop your bilateral stimulation.

6. What disturbance came to mind?

    _____

    _____

    _____

7. How did this disturbance show up for you? For example, perhaps it was merely a thought, or perhaps it showed up as a certain color or image, or maybe it was a specific situation, person, or body sensation.

    _____

    _____

    _____

8. Begin your bilateral stimulation again, and continue with it as you envision the disturbance you identified. As you do, imagine putting this disturbance inside your container. Notice the way you would open your container, and envision securely leaving this disturbance safely inside. Continue with your bilateral stimulation until you feel comfort and a sense of distance from the disturbance that is now stowed in your container.

9. Taking another deep breath and resuming your bilateral stimulation, notice that all of your distress and worry surrounding this disturbance is being safely stored inside your container and will remain there until you feel ready to process whatever you placed inside.

10. Stop your bilateral stimulation, and take a deep breath in as you allow yourself to notice the relief that you just experienced. How does that feel?

    _____

    _____

    _____

Note: If you have difficulty placing certain thoughts or disturbances inside the container, it may be helpful for you to repeat this exercise. When you get to the prompt of placing something inside, you can imagine giving these more difficult images or thoughts to someone you trust who could carefully place them inside your container for you.

It is natural to become stuck and feel unable to place certain things inside the container. When this happens, use a mental support from your restoration team or use the added imagery of something else shouldering this burden for you.

If you asked someone to help you place items into the container, who was this resource?

_____

At times, you may find it difficult to keep items inside your mental container. If this happens, you can repeat this exercise and imagine a person you trust putting a passcode or lock on your container or simply giving your container to someone you trust until you are ready to address these disturbances. You can be creative and imaginative within your own process.

This exercise can be useful to move day-to-day disturbances out of your mind and provide temporary relief of burdens you are carrying. You can use this anytime you wish to move worries, thoughts, fears, anxieties, situations, people, triggers, and so on out of the forefront of your mind. This will help you to feel more present in your day-to-day circumstances and often offers comfort for the time being (Parnell 2018).

The aim of the Container Exercise is not to dissociate or forget what has taken place in your life; it is merely a holding zone and safe space to allow your brain refuge from all that it carries. In the next chapter, I will guide you on how to revisit the objects in your container so that they can have the time and attention they deserve to truly be healed.

When you encounter triggers related to your trauma, I suggest returning to this exercise and putting the trigger, worry, event, or memory inside the container. You can even envision unlocking the container and then relocking it once you have completed the exercise each time. You can also place in your container any disturbances that arise as you engage in this workbook so that you can address and fully process these issues when the time is right.

Due to the nature of this exercise and to prevent avoidance, I strongly suggest that you keep a working log of things that you envision placing inside your container. I recommend noting the date, disturbance, and intensity of what you placed inside your container, as shown in the example below. This will help you identify things you would like to address in your healing journey and ensure that nothing gets left behind.

Container Tracking Log

Date	Disturbance	Level of Disturbance (1–10, where 1 = Low and 10 = High)
1/19	Disagreement with coworker	4

Now that you have learned ways to find and build resources as you work on healing your past painful experiences and triggers, let's proceed on your EMDR journey. Thank you for allowing me to be your guide.

CHAPTER FOUR

Explore Your Past Trauma and Core Beliefs

Do the best you can until you know better. Then when you know better, do better.

—Maya Angelou

Tanya was one of my most cherished clients. Her spirit would light up a room with just her smile. She was highly educated, hardworking, and beautiful, and she carried herself with confidence, joy, and enthusiasm. When I first met Tanya, I was surprised by her initial presentation, as she had been referred to my office by her probation officer for driving under the influence for the second time. She bounced into my office with a jubilant greeting and heartfelt introduction, and I quickly realized that she knew how to present herself well and put on a mask that was expected and welcomed by society.

Tanya had a bachelor's degree, worked in management at a prestigious hotel chain, and was currently attending college for a second degree in substance abuse counseling. She was very knowledgeable about alcohol addiction and could tell me all about the collapse of her life to addiction. She knew all of her own causes, triggers, and relapse symptoms yet still had continued to wrestle within the throes of her addiction. She shared that she had never worked through her past traumatic experiences, specifically the ongoing struggle with an abusive live-in boyfriend that she had been unable to break free from. I knew that these underlying, unresolved traumas were a key ingredient in her constant struggle with addiction and that addressing them would be vital to breaking the cycle.

I had seen Tanya consistently for about two years. She maintained a good bout of sobriety during this time, but after a fight with her boyfriend, she relapsed on alcohol, isolated in her home. She reached out to me after a few days of bingeing, embarrassed and ashamed of her loss of control and her return to alcohol. After learning of her relapse, her probation officer requested that her probation be revoked and that she serve the remainder of her probation period in jail. She timidly asked me if I could come to court for the hearing, and I agreed.

At the court hearing, I listened as her probation officer described her as "a lost cause, someone who has been given more than enough opportunities to get sober but doesn't care enough to actually choose sobriety" and that she "would never change and should sit in jail due to her lack of effort." The judge responded in a similar tone, telling her how she had failed and shouldn't be given any more opportunities to gain sobriety. The reasons for her continued relapsing and struggles with sobriety finally clicked for me. She believed at her core that she was exactly who they described: a failure, that she would never change, and that she did not deserve second chances or to make mistakes. It was these deeply rooted core beliefs that led to her continued bouts of depression, shame, and substance use.

Outraged by the judge and probation officers' shaming and lack of education or understanding of how closely related trauma and addiction are, I asked to speak on behalf of my client. The judge granted my request and I addressed the courtroom. I told them that I would drink too if I was constantly told that I was a failure, not worth any more chances, and bound to screw up. I emphasized that if I were surrounded by people who were telling me I was a lost cause and hopeless, I would be in the same place as she was. I went on to explain the link between trauma and addiction and all the progress we had been making and her successes throughout the past two years. The judge listened intently and granted my request for her to remain in treatment and out of jail. As we left the courtroom that day, Tanya's eyes welled with tears. She told me I was the first person in her life to ever stand up for her, advocate for her, or say she was worth a chance.

You may not have an advocate in your life. If that is the case, I want you to know that we are in this together. I will be here on this journey with you, advocating for you until you can learn to advocate for yourself—and you will. It takes just one person advocating for or affirming us to become resilient and overcome our trauma. I hope that as you walk on your journey and I affirm you, you will find one other person who will do the same for you, and I sincerely hope that you will identify the people in your life whom *you* can also affirm.

Understanding Your Past Experiences

You have learned a lot about your symptoms in previous chapters. Now, you will shift to understanding what may have caused some of these symptoms. We will start with exploring some of your early childhood experiences. Although some or all of these experiences may not be relevant, I encourage you to read this section to ensure that you are not overlooking any of these early experiences.

You may be wondering why early childhood experiences are essential for you to identify. Simply put, it is because a lot of your adult identity is impacted by the first eighteen years of your life. That was when your brain was growing and developing amid particular environmental conditions and relationship attachments that you experienced. To identify your early experiences, we will be using a tool called the Adverse Childhood Experience (ACE) questionnaire, which lists ten types of childhood trauma. Since 1990, the Centers for Disease Control and Prevention (CDC) has studied adverse childhood experiences, often referred to as ACEs. The CDC has found that these adverse childhood experiences directly impact your overall health, risk for death, and risk for developing certain diseases, including mental illness and substance use disorders (www.CDC.gov/vitalsigns/aces/index.html). Let's look at what the research shows to make this feel more real:

- At least 67% percent of the US population has experienced at least one of the scenarios listed on the ACE questionnaire.

- In addition, one in five people in the United States today report having at least three or more of the experiences listed on the ACE questionnaire.

- Five of the top ten leading causes of death today in the United States are directly linked to how many of these events found on the ACE questionnaire a person has experienced and/or endured.

- People who have encountered four or more of these ACEs are seven times more likely to abuse substances, twelve times more likely to commit suicide, and four and a half times more likely to develop depression (Centers for Disease Control and Prevention 2019).

These results, which are common across all demographic groups, validate the significant impact that trauma has in our lives. Although the ACE questionnaire does not encompass all types of trauma we may have experienced, or the impact of trauma that occurs in adulthood, it gives us a general understanding as to how these earlier experiences shape our responses, beliefs, and trust in ourselves and others.

Trauma and PTSD impact every part of you: your body, your mind, your spirit, and your world. These changes do not have to be permanent. Knowledge is power, and when we gain knowledge about ourselves and our experiences, we can create a new future and provide hope to others along the way who have felt similarly to us. So take a deep breath and engage this source of self-knowledge.

The Adverse Childhood Experience Questionnaire

This questionnaire contains questions about events that happened during the first eighteen years of your life. The information you provide by answering these questions will allow you to better understand the traumas that may have occurred early in your life and explore how these experiences have shaped your beliefs about yourself, others, and the world around you (National Center for Injury Prevention and Control, Division of Violence Provision 2021).

Please answer each question by simply checking Yes or No.

During your first eighteen years of life:

1. Did a parent or other adult in the household often:

    Swear at you, insult you, put you down, or humiliate you?

    Or

    Act in a way that made you afraid that you might be physically hurt?

    ☐ YES   ☐ NO

2. Did a parent or other adult in the household often:

    Push, grab, slap, or throw something at you?

    Or

    Ever hit you so hard that you had marks or were injured?

    ☐ YES   ☐ NO

3. Did an adult or person at least five years older than you ever:

    Touch or fondle you or have you touch their body in a sexual way?

    Or

    Attempt or actually have oral, anal, or vaginal intercourse with you?

    ☐ YES   ☐ NO

4. Did you often feel that:

    No one in your family loved you or thought you were important or special?

    Or

    Your family didn't look out for each other, feel close to each other, or support each other?

    ☐ YES   ☐ NO

5. Did you often feel that:

   You didn't have enough to eat, had to wear dirty clothes, and had no one to protect you?

   Or

   Your parents were too drunk or high to take care of you or take you to the doctor if you needed it?

   ☐ Yes   ☐ No

6. Were your parents ever separated or divorced? ☐ Yes   ☐ No

7. Were any of your parents or other adult caregivers:

   Often pushed, grabbed, slapped, or had something thrown at them?

   Or

   Sometimes or often kicked, bitten, hit with a fist, or hit with something hard?

   Or

   Ever repeatedly hit over at least a few minutes or threatened with a gun or knife?

   ☐ Yes   ☐ No

8. Did you live with anyone who was a problem drinker or alcoholic, or who used street drugs?

   ☐ Yes   ☐ No

9. Was a household member depressed or mentally ill, or did a household member attempt suicide?

   ☐ Yes   ☐ No

10. Did a household member go to prison? ☐ Yes   ☐ No

Scoring

When scoring, count each Yes answer as one (1) point. The total number of Yes answers determines your individual ACE Score.

   ACE SCORE: _____

I know that this exercise can bring up a lot of emotions and difficult memories. I want to take a moment to check in with how you are doing after considering these experiences. If you are feeling troubled, or memories are surfacing, consider putting them in your container (as you learned in chapter three) for now. Or you may desire to use Calm Place or one of the other exercises you have learned so far. You'll find audio recordings of these, and others, at http://www.newharbinger.com/49586. Choose whatever feels right for you. If you do decide to use the Container Exercise, please record this experience on your Container Tracking Log.

Note the coping exercise you chose: _____

I'd like you to take a moment and write about how you are doing now. Let's start by getting in touch with your senses.

I can see this in my environment: _____

_____

_____

I can hear this around me: _____

_____

_____

Right now, I feel these sensations in my body: _____

_____

_____

Next, reflect on the emotions you're experiencing.

These emotions are coming up for me: _____

_____

_____

This is how I am feeling about my healing journey right now: _____

_____

_____

Whether you had any experiences listed in the ACE questionnaire or not, it is important for you to understand and acknowledge how impactful these earlier years can be. The early years of life are when you learn how to interpret the world, develop your self-perception, have (or don't have) your basic needs met, and learn how to interact with others. Our need for relationship attachment has been found to be as crucial to our survival as shelter and food. From the moment you are born, you quickly learn if it is safe to attach to, trust, or depend on others. This trust and dependence will be determined based on whether others notice you, respond to your needs, and care for you with recognition, love, and support.

The Impact of Trauma and PTSD on Relationships

We all seek safety and self-acceptance. It is as innate as survival. And anytime your safety and self-acceptance are threatened, such as in experiences you may have identified in the ACE questionnaire or experiences in adulthood, you will naturally seek to avoid any similar threats in the future. This avoidance of painful experiences is natural. However, when we seek to distract or restrict ourselves, we can create rigid tendencies in our lives that operate as safety mechanisms.

Even though some of these rigid tendencies have aided you, they also likely resulted in your becoming more inflexible and set in your behaviors, making it difficult to cope with change or things outside of your routine or comfort zone. These rigid behaviors, a maladaptive survival skill, tend to force you to function as either fully independent or codependent (i.e., excessively reliant on another person for your self-worth). This means that, given your past negative experiences or relationships, you either

1. feel that you cannot trust others (you insist you must fully rely on yourself—and no one else—to avoid rejection, hurt, or pain) or

2. feel that you cannot trust yourself (you become hypervigilant and insecure; you rely on everyone else for security and answers).

Do you recognize yourself in these descriptions? Write about which style feels more familiar to you, independent or codependent.

_____

_____

_____

Write one example of how you act in either an independent or codependent way in your daily life.

_____

_____

_____

Oftentimes, this rigid thinking prevents you from finding the middle ground and keeps you out of balance with yourself. In order to find balance within your internal physical system, self, and relationships, interdependence must occur.

Interdependence is the ability to recognize your abilities and strengths and trust your insight while also acknowledging your limits, your restrictions, and the fact that you do not have all the answers. In interdependence, you are self-reliant and do what you are able to do, and you also rely on others or ask for help when needed. You are safe to express vulnerability and establish boundaries, not just with others but with yourself as well.

Finding this level of interdependence will be a task that you can practice along this journey. I believe that your willingness to search for answers and learn new information is a sign of interdependence. The more willing you are to recognize your limits, restrictions, and rigid behaviors, the easier your healing process will be and the fewer blocks you will run into along the way.

Core Beliefs

Much of your identity and self-worth comes from early interactions with others. Your relationships with others in the world around you lead to forming negative or positive beliefs about yourself, which we refer to as "core beliefs." We also form core beliefs as we encounter pivotal events in our lives. If you tend to have negative beliefs about yourself, reprocessing them, or rediscovering a new meaning, will be pivotal in your healing. As you learn to adopt more positive ways of thinking about yourself, you will begin to encode new adaptive information in your brain's processing center and expand your once held limiting views.

You have probably spent a lot of time trying to understand and make meaning of the "whys" in your life. *Why did this happen to me? Why did I have to suffer? Why can't I control my emotions? Why do people hurt me? Why do I feel more intensely than others? Why was I left?* The list could continue. You might be searching for the meaning behind the pain and confusing circumstances you have encountered in your life, hoping that with this understanding you will finally be able to free some of the pain and shame that you carry.

Within you lie deeply rooted values, feelings, emotions, and beliefs that guide and shape the way in which you operate and exist in your world. As mentioned above, your belief system often forms in the early years of life and is strongly influenced by your own personal experiences, interpretations, and conclusions drawn, as well as what the people closest to you told you to be true. These early experiences play a major role in shaping the beliefs that you will form around yourself, others, and the world around you.

Your brain assigns meaning and significance to your relationships, events, and circumstances that you face. For example, if you graduate from high school, your brain may associate this with accomplishment and positive regard for yourself. However, perhaps you don't graduate and instead you receive your GED. Based on the messages you received about the importance of education, your brain may believe this to be a disappointing experience. The meaning that we assign to things contributes to our set of core beliefs. These beliefs become the inner dialogue that we tell ourselves regarding our limits, capabilities, and worth.

Negative Core Beliefs

Part of the EMDR framework involves identifying the negative beliefs you carry today because of the past events you have faced in your life. Negative beliefs are the interpretations you made about yourself at the time trauma occurred. For example, let's say your spouse had an ongoing affair during your marriage. When you learned of this occurring, perhaps you assigned a meaning about yourself (like *I am unlovable*). This belief that you formed because of your spouse's affair may still impact you today. Identifying your faulty, negative interpretations of yourself from your past traumatic experiences will help you identify parts of your life that need to be reprocessed or explored as a means to assist in changing these negative core beliefs that you hold about yourself. These negative core beliefs can be anything from believing that you are permanently damaged because of your difficulty in relationships to believing you are unsafe in the world around you because of your past experience of being present during a mass act of violence.

If you experienced trauma in childhood or adolescence, your brain was not developed enough for you to recognize alternative roads of survival. You did the best you could at the time. You used the skills you had and the information you knew. As you moved from childhood and adolescence into adulthood with these traumatic past experiences, you may have tightly clung to these once self-protective skills as this was all you knew. This may have involved isolating, numbing out with substances, picking fights, avoiding closeness, or dissociating, among other responses. You may have come to learn through early childhood experiences that you cannot express your needs, your feelings, or your own truth because doing so would often result in neglect, severe punishment, or rejection. You may have learned to hide and bury your own true self in order to survive and to ensure that you will have connection and not be rejected. I wonder what parts of your personality or character you have hidden, rejected, or abandoned because they were never seen, embraced, heard, or scrutinized. These are often the creative, hopeful, imaginative, and unique aspects of yourself.

Whatever you did to protect yourself and cope with your emotions was likely all you knew or what you had been taught to do. It is common for change to feel scary or unsafe. It may especially feel this way for you because the trauma you have faced has been uncertain or unpredictable. So when new situations come up or change is required, it can feel overwhelming. You may feel debilitating anxiety, fear of failing, or the urge to sabotage your own success to avoid future anticipated harm. Or the emotions that come up may seem too big or painful to rein in. I want you to know that these feelings and emotions are normal and that they will get easier as you continue to take each new step.

We all experience devastating times in our lives, and for some of us that may not occur until later in life. These experiences can have a staggering impact on the way we perceive and operate in the world around us. When these traumatic occurrences happen in our adult life, they can impact our core beliefs, creating huge shifts in our psyche and our ability to feel safe, trust others, and trust ourselves. But even if you have faced uncertain times that have greatly impacted your life, you can still reclaim your senses of self-worth and security.

Here is the time line of how a negative core belief cascades in any moment, with an example.

1. Upsetting event (someone turned down a dinner invitation)

2. Reaction or what you did (*I felt rejected and embarrassed*)

3. The expectation you had or what you thought would happen (*I thought they liked me and would want to go out to dinner with me*)

4. The negative message you hold about this expectation (*I am only worthy if I am accepted*)

5. The myths and assumptions you are making (*I must be accepted by others to feel worthy*)

6. The core belief (*Who I am is not worthy of others' acceptance*)

Now, see if you can perceive how this plays out in your life. Track an upsetting event that triggered your negative core beliefs.

1. Upsetting event: _____

_____

_____

2. Reaction or what you did: _____

    _____

    _____

3. The expectation you had or what you thought would happen: _____

    _____

    _____

4. The negative message you hold about this expectation: _____

    _____

    _____

5. The myths and assumptions you are making: _____

    _____

    _____

6. The core belief: _____

    _____

    _____

Now do it one more time, with a different upsetting event.

1. Upsetting event: _____

    _____

    _____

2. Reaction or what you did: _____

    _____

    _____

3. The expectation you had or what you thought would happen: _____

    _____

    _____

4. The negative message you hold about this expectation: _____

    _____

    _____

5. The myths and assumptions you are making: _____

    _____

    _____

6. The core belief: _____

    _____

    _____

Perhaps you have felt stuck—even when you have come to conclusions about "why" your past experiences happened. Part of why this occurs is because trauma changes your perceptions and belief system. In order to rewrite and unlink some of your negative beliefs and perceptions, it is important for you to understand the way in which your brain has determined some of these thoughts. Be encouraged that these underlying core beliefs that you carry can and will change as you continue to do your own work.

Positive Core Beliefs

Let's now discuss the core beliefs we utilize in EMDR. The beliefs we hold about ourselves, others, and the world around us can be deeply rooted in the experiences we have had. The meaning we give these experiences will often shape the beliefs we form about ourselves. If you are like me, you have likely wrestled with having positive regard for yourself or have doubted yourself and your worth. One of the most empowering pieces of EMDR is redefining the way you see and feel about yourself.

Here is a list of positive core beliefs, adapted from work by Francine Shapiro (2018), that are used in conjunction with EMDR therapy. Take a moment and identify the beliefs you have about yourself by underlining them. Then circle the beliefs that you *would like to* feel about yourself.

I DESERVE LOVE OR I CAN HAVE LOVE.

I AM A GOOD/LOVING PERSON.

I AM FINE AS I AM.

I AM WORTHY OR I AM WORTHWHILE.

I AM HONORABLE.

I AM LOVABLE.

I AM DESERVING.

I AM OKAY.

I DESERVE GOOD THINGS.

I AM OR CAN BE HEALTHY.

I AM FINE AS I AM.

I CAN HAVE OR DESERVE...

I AM INTELLIGENT.

I AM ABLE TO LEARN.

I AM SIGNIFICANT.

I AM IMPORTANT.

I DESERVE TO LIVE.

I DESERVE TO BE HAPPY.

I AM OKAY JUST THE WAY I AM.

I DID THE BEST I COULD.

I AM SAFE NOW.

I LEARNED (CAN LEARN) FROM IT.

I DO THE BEST I CAN.

I CAN BE TRUSTED.

I CAN (LEARN TO) TRUST MYSELF.

I CAN (LEARN TO) TRUST MY JUDGMENT.

I CAN CHOOSE WHOM TO TRUST.

I CAN TAKE CARE OF MYSELF.

I CAN SUCCEED.

I CAN SAFELY FEEL MY EMOTIONS.

I CAN MAKE MY NEEDS KNOWN.

I AM STRONG.

I CAN CHOOSE TO LET IT OUT.

I AM NOW IN CONTROL.

I NOW HAVE CHOICE.

I CAN GET WHAT I WANT.

I CAN BE MYSELF.

I CAN MAKE MISTAKES.

I CAN HANDLE IT.

I AM CAPABLE.

Like me, you may long to feel positive regard toward yourself but are unsure why this seems so difficult. Even if your circled phrases outnumber your underlined phrases, awareness of where you're headed supports your healing. One way to begin to develop positive core beliefs is to start with some self-compassion. First, recognize that your past traumatic experiences may have given you the strength to endure things beyond your own comprehension or control. Honor that these past survival skills you have used served a purpose, but just like training wheels on a bike, there comes a time where they are no longer needed. To embrace this journey of change, ease the intensity of emotions you may feel, and find new ways to attach to others, it will be necessary to acknowledge and show yourself compassion, as we learned in chapter three.

Let's take a moment and practice showing yourself grace and support. I would like you to identify some statements of compassion, specifically in areas where you typically feel shame or judgment toward yourself. For example, a statement of compassion might be "I did the best I could" or "I didn't know any better."

Write down three statements of compassion for yourself.

1. _____

2. _____

3. _____

Next, we'll do an EMDR exercise to help you embrace positive beliefs about yourself.

Learn to Embrace Yourself

This exercise is available in an audio format, which you can download at http://www.newharbinger. com/49586.

Select the type of bilateral stimulation that you will be using for this exercise: eye movements, butterfly hug, knee tapping, or auditory stimulation. Remember to choose whichever bilateral stimulation method works for you and makes you feel comfortable. I will tell you when to add the bilateral stimulation and when to stop using it. When I prompt you to use the bilateral stimulation, you will do it for approximately 30–60 seconds.

1. Take a moment and list some of your characteristics, dreams, passions, or imaginative personality traits that you remember having from childhood or traits you developed during adolescence or even as an adult. Think specifically about traits, characteristics, or passions that you have left behind in your life (e.g., love for adventure, passion for helping others, desire to create new things). Write them down.

   _____

   _____

   _____

   _____

   _____

2. Now, take a moment and reflect on what it would take for you to accept these characteristics, traits, dreams, or passions that you listed. Begin your form of bilateral stimulation and continue with it for approximately 30–60 seconds as you consider this question.

Breathing in and out, reflect on what came to mind during that set of processing. Write down what is arising for you.

_____

_____

_____

_____

3. Once more, begin your bilateral stimulation, and now reflect on what you would need in order to accept these different aspects or characteristics of yourself that you long to embrace. Continue with this imagery for approximately 30–60 seconds.

    What did you observe that would allow you to embrace these parts of yourself?

    _____

    _____

    _____

    _____

4. Taking a deep breath in and resuming your bilateral stimulation, envision embracing these unique strengths within yourself. Furthermore, if you embraced these characteristics within yourself, consider how they would contribute to helping you heal. Continue with your bilateral stimulation for approximately 30–60 seconds.

5. Once you stop your bilateral stimulation, identify one of these characteristics or traits that you will commit to utilizing during your healing journey (e.g., "I will be more creative and forgiving").

    On this healing journey, I commit to: _____

    _____

I want to commend you for the progress you are making. You have been brave and bold throughout the last few exercises and have faced past wounds and triggers. This is challenging work that you are persevering through.

Gaining Distance from Traumatic Memories

Do you ever get flashes of memories that seem to haunt you? Or find yourself triggered frequently by familiar cues of your trauma? Ninety-eight percent of flashbacks occur not because we are in danger but because we are experiencing a physical or emotional response that was associated with the root trauma. In a sense, it's as if we are re-experiencing the trauma. Furthermore, our brain tends to become habituated to our fight, flight, or freeze response if it has operated this way for a long time. The brain floods our body with adrenaline any time we are activated by our trauma.

One of the ways that you will begin to reclaim a sense of power and safety when flooded with flashbacks or trauma reminders is by creating some distance from the ways you re-experience these symptoms. A common way that this is done within EMDR is through the use of what we call *distancing strategies*. Distancing strategies can help you regain your focus on positive things in your current life instead of focusing on the negative triggers or reminders. This technique can help you regain control of your thoughts.

Let's do an exercise together to give you some practice using distancing strategies.

Choose Your Movie Clip

If you choose, you can download the audio recording of this exercise at http://www.newharbinger.com/49586. Once again, select the type of bilateral stimulation that you will be using for this exercise: eye movements, butterfly hug, knee tapping, or auditory stimulation. Remember to choose whichever bilateral stimulation method works for you and makes you feel comfortable. I will tell you when to add the bilateral stimulation and when to stop using it. When I prompt you to use the bilateral stimulation, you will do it for approximately 30–60 seconds.

1. First, I want you to imagine that you are sitting in an empty movie theater. You can choose to be alone in this space or to have people or objects of comfort sitting with you; either choice is perfectly fine.

2. Begin your bilateral stimulation as you imagine yourself sitting in a movie theater. As you do, I want you to imagine a reel of a time in your life beginning to play on the screen. Just notice as if you are simply an observer in the theater, watching a movie play out in front of you. After 30–60 seconds, stop your bilateral stimulation. Describe the movie you saw:

   _____

   _____

   _____

3. Breathing in and out, starting your bilateral stimulation again, bring up this image once more. As you envision this reel of time in your life on the movie screen in front of you, I want you to notice that you can stop, pause, fast-forward, or rewind the movie as you see fit. Imagine stopping the film on a favorite memory from your life. After 30–60 seconds you can stop your bilateral stimulation. Note here where you chose to stop your movie reel.

_____

_____

4. Consider this statement: *Ultimately, you have control over where your mind chooses to rest.* What might this mean for the memories or flashbacks that seem to haunt you? Write about what it would feel like to direct your own movies in your head.

_____

_____

_____

As we continue with our work on your journey through this workbook, it may be helpful for you to use this movie theater analogy as we bring up difficult things from your past. Feel free to return to this exercise and practice, using it to create a sense of distance or to remind yourself that you are in charge of your memories. You will find this to be a powerful tool moving forward as you continue to heal and work through traumatic incidences from your past. You are the director of your own movie and life.

CHAPTER FIVE

Reclaim Your Past, Present, and Future

This is your life, your story, your book. Let today be the day you no longer let anyone else write it; nor apologize for the edits you make.

—Steve Maraboli

Devon doesn't recall a time of peace in his early years. Rather, he grew up in a volatile and chaotic home environment without positive role models. His mother suffered from depression and PTSD, which resulted in a lack of mothering. His father was extremely abusive, both physically and emotionally. The family would frequently move due to his father's service in the military. Overall, there was no form of consistency or stability in Devon's childhood, and as a result, he grew up feeling as if he was never enough. He constantly sought approval from others and felt responsible for his father's explosive behaviors in the home. Internally, he was haunted with lingering beliefs that he was somehow to blame for his parents' mental instability, which he assumed meant that he must be unlovable or simply incapable of making others happy.

After graduating from high school, Devon left home and joined the military. He thought that he was free from the turmoil that he once endured and that maybe now he would finally feel desirable to others. But despite being out of his traumatic home environment, he still couldn't shake the negative feelings that he held about himself. They still were ever present in his mind. He would constantly compare himself to others, resulting in his feeling broken and unable to fully connect with others. He began to use alcohol as a way to cut loose and have fun. It allowed him the freedom to experience life and feel a sense of confidence that he never seemed able to have when sober. As life progressed for Devon, he found himself turning to alcohol to cope with everyday life stressors, including his first divorce.

Devon met his second wife while out drinking with friends at a local bar. He was sure that this newfound love would heal the pain he was desperately driven to hide. However, throughout this second marriage, his drinking became uncontrollable. He found himself using alcohol to cope with anxiety, connect to his wife, and avoid his poor self-image and the plague of insecurity he still felt. Years into this marriage, he learned of his wife's numerous affairs and was devastated and heartbroken. Once again, he was left feeling unwanted, unlovable, and insecure, causing him to spiral further into addiction and leaving him in a pit of despair for years to come.

Despite being a very successful, handsome, high-ranking government official, Devon had difficulty sitting with himself when sober. Each time he found himself with a clear mind, the shameful beliefs of being less than, screwed up, and insignificant came flooding back. As a result, to numb these painful thoughts, his drinking became completely out of control. His family lost hope. He lost hope and change seemed impossible.

After multiple hospitalizations and a long-term stay at an inpatient substance abuse treatment program, Devon realized that he could no longer continue down the path he was traveling without facing death. In fear of losing his life, he willingly made the choice to turn his life around and committed to Alcoholics Anonymous and treatment as a last-ditch effort to save himself.

Despite the difficulty coming to terms with his pain and trauma, Devon began to explore his deeply rooted internal negative beliefs that he had spent years trying to run from. He managed to crawl his way out of the bottle and embrace a new and authentic way of living.

Over time, Devon slowly began exploring the development of his feelings of self-loathing through reflecting on his childhood and the messages that were instilled in him from a young age. As he became more and more curious about himself and the lens in which he viewed things, he slowly began to identify the new ways he desired to feel about himself.

Fast forward to today. Devon is close to two years sober. He is full of life and a hope that he never thought he would find. The man once plagued with self-hate can now make eye contact, be vulnerable, and even talk with statements of compassion about himself and the negative experiences he has faced. Once incapable of admitting to his shortcomings, he now is able to recognize the lessons he acquired through each past experience, whether positive or negative. Most impressive is seeing the value he holds for himself as a person. This once tormented man who came close to death by the bottle now can see worth and meaning in his life. He has rebuilt relationships with his children, which were once lost, and has surrounded himself with people and supports that remind him of his worth. If you would have asked Devon two years ago if he thought change or being able to love himself was possible, he would have told you no. Yet, here he lives and thrives with joy and peace. His ability to find himself and truly embrace all the parts of himself is a living example that you can change the gut-wrenching beliefs you hold about yourself.

Like Devon, you can rid yourself of the negative beliefs that hold you back. You can be in control of the way you feel about yourself just as Devon learned to do. I want you to remember that you have the power to change your life and restore the value in it. You have no doubt faced negative events and experiences that have impacted your beliefs about yourself. Even though these narratives have had a lasting impact on your life, you can learn to redefine the meaning that they now hold.

In this chapter, I will teach you ways to overcome some of these internal barriers that have led you to form negative beliefs about yourself and reclaim your past, present, and future.

Learning to Accept Your Past

Looking back on past pain is uncomfortable. You may not want to be reminded of the hurt that was left behind. It is easier at times to avoid the discomfort. Here is the thing, though: comfort is always the enemy of progress. In order to experience change and growth, we will have to go through some difficult growing pains. If you are willing to look back, you will discover clues and evidence that will allow you to see things in a different light. And, most importantly, you will find that embracing your past trauma stops it from carrying forward.

Update Your Past Self

I want to introduce you to a useful exercise that will help you get unstuck from the past and be able to fully live in the present moment. The goal of this practice is to assist you with feeling more supported and to recognize the strengths, capabilities, and resources that you hold inside yourself today. You can practice this whenever you feel it is necessary or when you find yourself triggered from moments in your past.

You can download an audio recording of this exercise at http://www.newharbinger.com/49586. If you're not listening to the audio recording, it may be helpful for you to read through this exercise a few times until you are familiar with the steps and can do it easily from memory. It may also be helpful to make notes as you read through it the first time and connect with the sensations and imagery of this exercise.

Select the type of bilateral stimulation that you will be using for this exercise: eye movements, butterfly hug, knee tapping, or auditory stimulation. Remember to choose whichever bilateral stimulation method works for you and makes you feel comfortable. I will tell you when to add the bilateral stimulation and when to stop using it. When I prompt you to use the bilateral stimulation, you will do it for approximately 30–60 seconds.

To begin:

1. Find a comfortable, quiet place and position.

2. Now, I would like you to take a moment and imagine yourself as a child. Envision an age that stands out and represents a time when you struggled with self-worth or experienced a lot of adversity. Note your age at the time and what came to mind. This could be times you felt fearful, insecure, or unsure of your future.

_____

_____

_____

3. Once you have an image of yourself from the past in mind, close your eyes, take a deep breath in and out, and begin your method of bilateral stimulation. Continue with this as you focus on the image of your past younger self. After about 30 seconds, stop your bilateral stimulation and note whatever image came to mind, particularly noting what you envisioned with this image.

_____

_____

_____

4. Take another breath in and out, and begin your method of bilateral stimulation as you consider the image you conjured of your younger self. It may be helpful to think of including the following:

- Where did you envision yourself being?

- How old did you see yourself?

- What was the mood or emotional response of your younger self?

Continue with your bilateral stimulation for approximately 30–60 seconds before stopping.

5. Take a deep breath in and out. You may take a moment and jot down any answers that came to mind from the questions above.

- Where did you envision yourself being? _____

_____

- How old did you see yourself? _____

_____

- What was the mood or emotional response of your younger self? _____

_____

- Also describe how your body and mind are feeling, right now. _____

_____

6. Begin your bilateral stimulation again, and this time as you do, consider this image of your younger, past self. Notice how you felt about yourself then. After considering this, go ahead and stop your bilateral stimulation, taking several deep breaths in and out. How did you feel about yourself at that age?

_____

_____

7. Beginning your bilateral stimulation once more, notice yourself now as you are in the present. As you continue with your bilateral stimulation and hold this image of yourself today in your mind, notice if there is anything that your current, present self would want to say to your younger self.

- Is there something that your younger self faced that they needed to hear or have acknowledged? _____

_____

_____

- How does this younger version of yourself respond to what you tell them? _____

_____

_____

8. After you have described all you noticed or thought of, take a deep breath in and out and stop your bilateral stimulation. Close your eyes once more and, adding your bilateral stimulation, bring up the images of your current self and your past child self. This time, allow your

current self to show your younger self how far you have come since you were a child. Tell them all you have learned and accomplished and all you are capable of. Let this younger child self know that they are safe now and no longer have to be afraid or feel alone. After approximately 30–60 seconds, you can open your eyes and stop bilateral stimulation. Note what came to mind.

_____

_____

_____

_____

_____

9. Breathing in and out, begin your bilateral stimulation while you envision this image of yourself now in the present along with your past self. As you do, I want you to imagine that your current self is going to take your past self to a place that feels safe and free. You may even choose to bring your past self with you into the present, so that they can add more joy and peace to your life today. After 30–60 seconds, stop your bilateral stimulation. Where did you choose to take your younger self? Describe the details of the place.

_____

_____

_____

_____

_____

Take a moment and reflect on the last image above. Your younger past self does not have to stay trapped in the former pain of your life. When triggering events come up from earlier in your life, you can use this exercise and re-envision your past self being somewhere safe. It will help you get unstuck from the hold of past events on your current life.

I invite you to note any personal discoveries or realizations that you had from completing this activity. How will this exercise be useful to you and what hope does it inspire?

_____

_____

_____

_____

_____

Embracing the Present

Reclaiming the past, present, and future are intertwined. Sometimes, it can feel difficult to even embrace your current life when you are working to overcome so much. It is important for you to know that this is possible—you can be free from the luggage of your past and calm your worries about the future. You can't accomplish this, however, until you've learned to accept the past and embrace the present. The present moments in life are preparing the way for what lies ahead. In this section, I want to help you break free from whatever element of time you riffle with and teach you to fully stand tall in your present life. The focus of this section will be just that—embracing ourselves as we currently are. Doing so involves two key aspects: self-acceptance and resiliency.

Building Self-Acceptance

Consider the following questions.

What do you believe today about yourself?

_____

_____

_____

_____

_____

How did you come to believe these thoughts about yourself?

_____

_____

_____

_____

_____

When you have faced trauma, your brain may instinctually doubt itself. It may subconsciously teach you to doubt yourself and constantly be on guard in the world around you in an effort to ensure your survival and avoid similar future threats. When this happens, you might:

- start questioning your decisions,

- believe you are responsible for bad things that have happened to you,

- feel like you should have done more, or,

- at worst, believe that you will be forever damaged by the events and circumstances you have faced.

Circle the effects from the list above that you see happening in your mind.

The silver lining is that your biggest insights and miracles will come after your biggest challenges and heartache. It is in the difficult times that we come face to face with what is important in our lives. Some of the most empathetic, compassionate people I have ever encountered have also survived horrific things in their lives. Their pain taught them to love more deeply, to show more forgiveness and grace, to notice the unnoticeable. And do you know why? Because they know the pain of not being shown those acts.

Someone very dear once shared that "the good never feels as good without the bad." There is truth to this. For when we truly know the pit of despair, we have insurmountable grace for the blessings in our lives. We have higher levels of resilience when we share and are able to connect with others. Our imperfections link us together.

Three Statements of Resiliency

"Are you being consistent and persistent?" Kevin Hall, a mentor of mine, asked this question at a recent retreat that I attended. He explained that everything we want is right beyond our comfort zone. When we practice being consistent and persistent in applying what we are learning and trying positive things on a daily basis, our resiliency increases. With this in mind, there are three statements that are shown to build our ability to overcome difficulties and raise our self-confidence, allowing us to be more persistent and resilient. These statements, listed below, are positive affirming statements we make about ourselves. I challenge you to complete each of the statements for yourself.

The first statement involves acknowledging what is available (e.g., *I have people who care about me; I have learned coping skills and have a supportive therapist*):

1. I have _____

The second statement reflects your personal value (e.g., *I am worthy of love; I am worthy of respect*):

2. I am _____

The third statement reflects hope for the future (e.g., *I can achieve my goals; I can make a positive effort today*):

3. I can _____

Getting in the habit of making these statements daily will help you build hope and belief in yourself and strengthen your resiliency to face life's ongoing challenges. These statements will help you tap into what motivates you and what you have to look forward to. This simple exercise can shift your focus to a stance of empowerment and capabilities. I encourage you to use this exercise as a daily practice for building your self-esteem and regaining love for yourself. Start with saying these statements out loud to yourself, daily. You may then want to add journaling these three statements once per day, ideally first thing in the morning to shift your mindset to a positive place. Each week, notice what statements you have repeated from this daily practice, and be mindful of how your thoughts and beliefs in yourself begin to change.

I want to teach you to thrive, not just survive.

Facing the Future with Strength and Support

Brain scans show that the reward system of our brain, the part that motivates us to respond or continue with a behavior, is activated when people share their story with others. Stories hold power. They remind us that we are not alone. We can help others just by helping ourselves and learning to embrace our own story.

One of your biggest challenges will be the practice of asking for help. You have experienced trauma and may have learned that it is often not safe to ask others for help. Perhaps when you have tried, you have been met with rejection or criticism, and you have learned to deal with most of life and life's problems on your own.

Our willingness to ask for help is not only beneficial for ourselves; it also allows others to serve and feel needed, wanted, respected, and so forth. Think for a minute about how you feel when someone comes to you, shares their pain, and asks for support, a listening ear, or other kind of help. You most likely feel honored to have such trust extended to you. We rob others of the gift of feeling needed and seen when we refuse to ask for help. The right people will support us when we reach out for help.

Don't let anyone tell you what you cannot do. They do not know the quiet, silent struggles that you have overcome. They do not know your internal resilience, which has allowed you to persevere time and time again. They have not seen all the battles you have fought. They don't know you. The truth is you have already beaten the odds. You have already continued to fight, crawl, and run ahead in life when it seemed impossible. You are capable of more than you can even think and imagine, and once you begin to embrace all your internal strength, your potential will become endless.

When you live in your truth, you give permission for others to live and stand in their own truths. This rings true in the well-known word *namaste*, which means that the light in me honors the light in you. You are one of a kind … and so are they.

Call on Your Restoration Team to Offer New Beliefs

Remember your restoration team from chapter two? Once again, this exercise will focus on the supports and resources that you have in your life. You can download an audio recording of this exercise at http://www.newharbinger.com/49586.

Begin by revisiting each of the roles listed here and who or what would fit into each category. I encourage you to make additions from the initial exercise in chapter two, if you're aware of any. Repeating this exercise can help you maintain consistency and persistence. Oftentimes, without practicing these skills we forget to return to interventions that work for us. And because the restoration team offers support, insight, and encouragement, expanding this exercise will help you as you establish newfound resiliency and beliefs.

Ideal Self: Imagine your ideal future self once more. This is yourself as the person you wish to be—yourself at your best. Ask your ideal self to describe:

What they see in you as your gifts as a person: _____

_____

_____

What qualities they most appreciate about you: _____

_____

_____

What your potential is in the world: _____

_____

_____

What would make your dreams and goals for your life more possible: _____

_____

_____

Protectors: keep you safe, watch over you, stand up for you, and are strong when you feel weak. Ask your protectors to describe:

What your gifts are as a person: _____

_____

_____

What qualities they most appreciate about you: _____

_____

_____

What your potential is in the world: _____

_____

_____

What would make your dreams and goals more possible: _____

_____

_____

Nurturers: offer unconditional love, comfort, acceptance, compassion, and nonjudgment. Ask your nurturers to describe:

What your gifts are as a person: _____

_____

_____

What qualities they most appreciate about you: _____

_____

_____

What your potential is in the world: _____

_____

_____

What would make these dreams and goals you have for your life more possible: _____

_____

_____

Wise Figures: offer sound knowledge, assist you in finding wise answers, offer confidence and certainty, and don't lead you astray. Ask your wise figures to describe:

What your gifts are as a person: _____

_____

_____

What qualities they most appreciate about you: _____

_____

_____

What your potential is in the world: _____

_____

_____

What would make your dreams and goals that you have for your life possible: _____

_____

_____

Spiritual Figures: provide infinite wisdom, faith, and comfort and remind you that you are being watched over or are connected to something bigger than yourself. Ask your spiritual figures to describe:

What your gifts are as a person: _____

_____

_____

What qualities they most appreciate about you: _____

_____

_____

What your potential is in the world: _____

_____

_____

What would make the dreams and goals you have for your life possible: _____

_____

_____

Now that you have revisited these resources and called on all of the above figures in your restoration team, let's add some bilateral stimulation of your choosing and expand this exercise even further. Select the type of bilateral stimulation that you will be using for this exercise: eye movements, butterfly hug, knee tapping, or auditory stimulation. Remember to choose whichever bilateral stimulation method works for you and makes you feel comfortable. I will tell you when to add the bilateral stimulation and when to stop using it. When I prompt you to use the bilateral stimulation, you will do it for approximately 30–60 seconds.

1. Find a comfortable, quiet place and position.

2. Close your eyes and take a moment to just be present with yourself. Notice your particular thoughts, feelings, emotions, and even the sensations within your body. Just listen and observe as you tune into your inner world. After about 30 seconds, open your eyes.

   What did you notice? _____

   _____

3. Breathing in and out, while beginning your bilateral stimulation, bring up each of the figures on your restoration team. Continue with your bilateral stimulation as you imagine:

   • Your ideal self. Notice the strengths, confidence, joy, and resolve you would have in this ideal state.

   • Your protectors. Envision their strengths, how they would fight for you, stand up for you, and guard you.

   • Your nurturing figures. Feel the compassion, love, support, nonjudgment, and loyalty that they provide you.

   • Your wise figures, with their resolve, confidence, wisdom, support, and guidance.

   • Finally, imagine your spiritual figures. Notice their infinite wisdom, the connection they provide, the faith and healing they would give you.

4. Bring all these figures together. Imagine what they would do or say to you as you sit here in this moment. Ask them to remind you:

   • Who am I truly? _____

   _____

   _____

- What do I often forget about myself? _____

_____

_____

- What is a source of hope I can draw on? _____

_____

_____

Embrace their wisdom, love, support, protection, and guidance. Continue with your bilateral stimulation for another 30 seconds.

5. Take a deep breath in and stop your bilateral stimulation.

6. Reflect for a moment and record anything significant as well as what they said to you, offered you, or provided you with.

_____

_____

_____

_____

_____

7. Allow yourself another deep breath in and out, begin your bilateral stimulation, and this time envision your restoration team telling you what your three best qualities are. Just notice as you continue with this imagery for 30–60 seconds.

8. Take a deep breath in and out and stop your bilateral stimulation.

What three qualities did they describe?

i.   _____

ii.   _____

iii.   _____

Do you feel your confidence growing? If so, write about how that feels. If not, share just what obstacle you are facing.

_____

_____

_____

9. Breathing in and out once more, begin your bilateral stimulation as you envision sitting with your restoration team. As you do, imagine asking them: *How do these best qualities I hold come from surviving my past pain?*

    Just listen to what they offer as they show you how these positive traits of yours were enhanced and strengthened because of your past pain. Continue for 30–60 seconds and then stop your bilateral stimulation.

    What insights and realizations did your restoration team share about surviving your past pain?

    _____

    _____

    _____

    How were these best qualities of yours enhanced or strengthened by this pain?

    _____

    _____

You can utilize this and practice this exercise anytime you feel that you need additional validation or want to feel more connected to yourself. Use these resources on your restoration team to assist you as you gain strength, compassion, love, encouragement, wisdom, and grace within yourself as you move forward and learn to reclaim strength to face the future. They are here to remind you that you are enough and that you hold everything inside that you need to live the life you desire.

I hope you recognize that you have come so far and accomplished so much that you never thought was possible earlier in your life. You are capable of growing and learning to become all you are meant to be.

CHAPTER SIX

Create New Skills to Manage Your Triggers

You can't go back and make a new start, but you can start right now and make a brand new ending.

—James Sherman

Meieli was one of thirteen children born in a large religious family in a very rural, remote area. Growing up, money was scarce. Her parents ran their own logging business and often required the children to work alongside them, from as early as four years old. The siblings younger than four would be strapped and left in their car seats in the family car for hours on end while the rest of the family worked. Meieli's mother or an older child would go to the car every four hours to feed the younger children, but they were told not to comfort their siblings if they were crying because they needed to promptly return to work. If they took too long or complained about work, her mother would often beat them.

Along with expectations of manual labor, food was scarce. Frequently, Meieli and other siblings did not eat. Medical attention was seen as an inconvenience; she recalled even the most severe injuries being ignored. As a result, she and her siblings were forced into survival of the fittest. Everyone except for Meieli was out for themselves in their own effort to survive. Meieli reported that she was the one who always noticed her siblings' pain. She would often take the blame for things that she had not done in an effort to protect her siblings from physical beatings. She would give food to others and care for those around her in an effort to make sure no one felt as she did—alone.

As a result of years of abuse and neglect, Meieli internalized the message that she was unworthy of love, care, and attention. As she developed, she carried these intrinsic messages about her worth and lack of value. Even though she was extremely caring and loving toward *others, she struggled to see herself as deserving of this love. Years later, she was still rife with the same feelings that she had fought and confronted as a child.*

Through counseling, Meieli came to the realization that she was fearful of rejection and abandonment; this was learned from years of burying her true self and having her needs ignored. She learned that not making her needs known, in her younger years and adult years, was her effort to protect those around her. In fact, most of her true identity, which resounded in caring for and loving others, was often shamed and ridiculed by her parents, even as an adult woman. Through her processing, she soon discovered how amazing it was that she had been able to give that amount of love amid the worst of times. She went on to realize that her acts of love and kindness were in fact innate, as they were not taught to her. She recognized that even though she was neglected and abused for most of her early years, the most important part of her—her kind, gracious heart—remained intact. Not even the abuse could steal who she is.

Ultimately, through her own EMDR treatment, Meieli arrived at the conclusion that she was finally safe to explore and express all of the unique capabilities, dreams, and passions she had once abandoned. She had to learn to get in touch with herself, not just on an emotional level but on a physical level as well, to understand why some of the manifestations and triggers from her past still occurred, and how to overcome them.

When Trauma Resurfaces

When memories or reminders of your past trauma occur, it is often not because you are in danger. You may instead be experiencing a somatic (body sensation) response or an emotion that was associated with something in the past that caused you to feel emotionally or physically unsafe. When this occurs, your brain often responds quickly if it is used to having to operate this way, as is the case with PTSD.

These reminders in your brain can seem to play on repeat, like a bad song you can't get out of your head. Part of why this occurs is because your brain stores negative, threatening experiences in such a way that they are readily accessible in an effort to keep you safe in the future. Your brain holds onto these experiences and will recall them if you experience anything associated with them. For example, you could smell the odor of oil at a gas station and be taken back to a car accident you experienced years earlier in which the smell of oil from the crash was overwhelming. The smell of oil again in the future tells your brain, "Hey, we are in danger because the last time we smelled oil we got seriously injured."

Getting these triggers and sensory reminders of this trauma unstuck is possible and will be addressed as we move forward in this chapter. And just like Meieli, you can learn to identify, address, and reframe these stuck memories and beliefs. First, let's examine the coping behaviors you currently use.

Seeing Through Coping Behaviors

Self-protective skills such as isolating, numbing out with substances, detaching by watching endless hours of TV, and avoiding close relationships are just a few examples of how you may have learned to endure the pain and shield yourself from more heartache. These protective skills served their purpose in keeping you safe from anticipated future pain. I want you to take a moment to acknowledge some of the different ways you may have taught yourself to cope through your pain.

Circle the behaviors or habits from the list below that you have used to find temporary relief from the pain of your trauma and PTSD. Simply circle the ones that apply to you. Feel free to use the spaces provided to write in any additional coping behaviors that you have turned to for coping.

Self-Protective Activities

Drinking alcohol

Gambling

Engaging in adrenaline-seeking behaviors

Using illicit drugs or abusing medications

Shopping

Daydreaming or spacing out

Sleeping for extended periods of time

Isolating from others

Overeating/binge eating

TV, social media, video games

Reading excessively

Overworking

Sex

Pornography

_____

_____

_____

_____

_____

_____

What can occur as a result of traumatic experiences is your ongoing use of these protective activities. But they no longer need to serve you. You may still avoid closeness with others or numb difficult emotions by drinking or overeating. Or perhaps you are constantly waiting for the other shoe to drop, and as a result find yourself still feeling emotional, anxious, or unsettled.

Let's take a moment to identify the ways your self-protective activities have become maladaptive. Answer these questions to identify how these behaviors have become disruptive in your life or been used in an effort to avoid unpleasant feelings or emotions.

1. When do you typically engage in the behaviors you identified from the list above?

    Examples:

    "I drink when I quit taking care of myself and start feeling overwhelmed with emotions."

    "I stop communicating with others in my life when I begin to feel like I will be hurt or rejected."

    _____

    _____

    _____

    _____

2. What is your first memory of using the behaviors you identified? How old were you?

    Example:

    "I began drinking when I was 12 after my friends encouraged me to 'let loose' at a party."

    _____

    _____

    _____

    _____

3. What relief did you experience after this first time using these behaviors? How did it help you at the time?

    _____

    _____

    _____

4. What negative repercussions have you experienced from continuing to engage in these activities?

_____

_____

_____

5. What skills do you wish you would have learned or been taught instead that you feel would have helped you cope?

_____

_____

_____

6. Why do you consider the behaviors you identified to be disruptive to you now? How do they get in the way of what you truly want?

_____

_____

_____

7. What healthy alternatives have you learned and developed—or are you aware of—since these earlier experiences that you could apply now?

_____

_____

_____

Notice from your answers that you were not trying to be reckless or careless. You were just trying to manage and survive in the best way you knew how.

When you have endured difficult events in life, your brain stores the experienced sensations of these events and draws from them in an ongoing effort to protect you. Your brain is acting like your smoke detector to signal future anticipated threats and danger. Through EMDR, you can help your brain learn to relax and release some of the information it previously stored as being dangerous that is no longer threatening you. You have been helping your brain to do this as you have been learning and engaging in all the exercises taught throughout this book. As you do this, you will find freedom from these habitual responses formed from past survival efforts and will find new, more beneficial mechanisms to cope with your feelings and emotions.

Remember that as scary as change may feel, through this workbook you are discovering different choices that you have now. As you continue to engage in these exercises and explore your past with curiosity, you may learn that some of your earlier painful experiences can become stepping-stones to developing new coping strategies.

Replacing Past Coping Behaviors with New Skills

You have no doubt been given the strength to endure things beyond your own comprehension or control. I can say this because you find yourself here, reading these pages. You have endured the most unfortunate events and circumstances. The level of strength and resiliency that it took you to live through these painful experiences is more than most people have. You are strong. You are a fighter. You are able to endure the unthinkable. You never give up.

And…you have the capability to adapt, try new things, and learn new ways to cope. In the next exercise, you will have an opportunity to give yourself compassion for the work you have done to cope with your pain thus far. Then, you'll explore reasons you may have had that coping response, and finally, new ways you might cope differently now and in the future.

Below, write down statements of compassion for the ways you have coped. For example, maybe it would help you to state that you did the best you could. Or perhaps it would help you to acknowledge that you are learning new ways to keep yourself safe. Whatever you choose is right for you and likely something you are needing to validate.

_____

_____

_____

Now, I invite you to apply this self-compassion to past situations. Below, identify some of the coping strategies you used at the time your trauma occurred.

How did you cope when the traumatic event(s) occurred?

Example: "I picked fights at school with my peers because I had so much anger inside."

_____

_____

What was your motivating belief or feeling at the time of this event?

Examples:

"I cannot stand the feelings inside me."

"It is not safe to talk about it."

_____

_____

What coping skill could you use now?

Example: "I can express my feelings to someone I trust who can help me sort through my feelings without lashing out."

_____

_____

What is the belief you would like to remember now to help you use this new coping skill?

Examples:

"I can safely express my feelings."

"I can let others help."

_____

_____

I hope that as you wrote your responses you were able to acknowledge the new skills and tools that you have in your life today. You are learning to develop and advance past your trauma and PTSD and have much more knowledge and insight than you did before. You will continue to make new discoveries and develop greater strengths as you move forward with your healing.

The Courage to Share Who You Are

Perhaps you have learned to hide and bury your own needs or your deepest thoughts and feelings. When you experience trauma, it is easy to abandon yourself in an effort to survive emotionally and physically. I wonder what parts of your self you have hidden, rejected, or abandoned because of the pain you have faced? Have you considered that these hidden or abandoned parts of yourself are likely some of your greatest attributes?

Take a moment and think of some of your earlier characteristics, dreams, passions, or personality traits that you remember from your childhood or adolescence. These could be things you have always wanted to try or secretly been curious about. You may have buried, denied, rejected, or abandoned them because you did not have the opportunity or encouragement to explore them. Reflect below on a few of the unique passions, abilities, or characteristics that you had as a child or adolescent. For example, this could be an ability to draw or sing, knowledge about animals or other topics, love of certain hobbies, or even having a large creative imagination. Reflect below on some of these unique interests or characteristics that you can recall.

_____

_____

_____

_____

_____

I want to challenge you to share one of these traits with someone closest to you, someone you trust. Share with them that you are learning to get back in touch with the unique parts of yourself that you have closed off, forgotten, or been afraid to share. Simply share with them and consider asking them for encouragement as you learn to embrace and acknowledge these important parts of yourself.

As you move forward with this practice, take a moment and reflect on what it would take for you to accept or explore these characteristics, traits, dreams, or passions.

What are the dreams or passions that may still be worth pursuing or exploring for yourself? For example, perhaps you have always enjoyed writing poetry but haven't done so in years.

_____

_____

_____

What holds you back from exploring these?

_____

_____

_____

Is there something new you would like to try that you have never allowed yourself the privilege of doing? For example, maybe you have always had a love for animals and would like to volunteer at an animal shelter.

_____

_____

_____

How might you share these interests with a certain person or group?

_____

_____

_____

Healing Creatively

Creativity has been found to be healing in and of itself. It can expand the landscape of your mind, create meaning where words are difficult to find, and lower your anxiety and depression. Just as you considered your dreams, hopes, and passions from earlier in your life, I want you to consider the creative parts of yourself that you still hold.

Embrace Your Creativity

I invite you to do an exercise that will help you to embrace the creativity within yourself. If you wish, you can download an audio recording of this exercise at http://www.newharbinger.com/49586.

To begin:

1. Find a comfortable, quiet place and position.

2. Close your eyes, if you feel comfortable doing so, and take a big deep breath in and out.

3. In your comfortable position, with your eyes open or closed, start by simply envisioning a plain, white canvas portrait.

4. As you envision the white canvas, notice that next to the canvas is a vast supply of different paint colors—every color you can imagine.

5. Notice that the canvas portrait is blank, ready for you to paint, create, and bring to life with all the paints or other supplies you can access in your imagination.

6. Imagine painting, drawing, or creating your own work of art on the canvas. It can be anything your mind envisions.

7. As you envision this work of art, no matter what comes to mind, just notice the unique, creative object that your mind conjured and created. Notice how unique and expansive you are.

8. Continue to just envision this image in your mind for 30–60 seconds.

9. Take a deep breath in and out and document below anything that stood out to you in this visualization. What went on your imaginary canvas?

_____

_____

_____

_____

_____

You are capable of tapping into the creative parts of your mind. Sometimes this takes practice and guidance; however, it will get easier as you practice the exercises in this book. As you learn to explore the inner workings of your beautiful mind, you will find it is easier to embrace these inner qualities of yourself with less shame.

Engaging the Brain-Body Connection to Feel More Calm

You have learned that you are hardwired for survival: not just your physical survival but that of your mind as well. When you are triggered or face trauma, your entire system—body and mind—will respond in an effort to protect you. Your brain and body have ongoing communication with each other to respond as necessary to whatever you may face.

For example, fear is a life-saving emotion that signals danger and allows us to protect ourselves and stay safe. If you are out hiking in the forest and encounter a rattlesnake, fear will kick on in your brain and prepare you to respond. Fear is necessary in situations like this to help you assess circumstances that could potentially be dangerous. Ultimately, fear is your brain and body's way of working together to protect you.

When you have experienced trauma, your brain will interpret the sensation or feelings linked to fear as danger, even when a situation is not in fact dangerous. As a result, your brain will tell your body to respond to this fear and send a release of stress hormones and adrenaline in an effort to prepare it to fight, flee, or freeze. When you experience stressful circumstances or events that are potentially emotionally or physically dangerous, your brain tells your body to prepare to respond. This is great for moments of survival, but ultimately, if left unresolved, can cause your body to stay overly alert or tense waiting to protect itself from any future threat or danger. This is what occurs with PTSD. Long after the trauma, the symptoms you experience are your body's protective fight, flight, or freeze responses in action, affecting you both mentally and physically.

Your brain and your body are close allies; they work hard to protect one another. If your brain is stressed, your body will be stressed, and vice versa. Experiences of pain and trauma commonly teach you to turn away from the feelings in your bodies, and you may feel unsafe noticing some of your own physical sensations. In the next section, we'll focus on how to understand and manage occurrences when your brain and body act in unexpected or seemingly out-of-control ways.

Shift Away from Triggers

I would like to walk you through an activity that will help you work through some of the triggers that cause your body and brain to respond the way that they do. You can also find an audio recording of this exercise at http://www.newharbinger.com/49586. I'll ask you to select a specific event from your past to focus on. Be gentle with yourself; this is an opportunity for you to learn more about yourself and your reactions.

Select the type of bilateral stimulation that you will be using for this exercise: eye movements, butterfly hug, knee tapping, or auditory stimulation. Remember to choose whichever bilateral stimulation method works for you and makes you feel comfortable. I will tell you when to add the bilateral stimulation and when to stop using it. When I prompt you to use the bilateral stimulation, you will do it for approximately 30–60 seconds.

1. I'd like you to think back on a disturbance from your life. Start with a mild event, not a major trauma. For example, this could be your parents' divorce earlier in your life and not being able to see one of your parents as much as a result. Or it could be having acne in school and being picked on for your appearance. Choose something that has caused some disruption to your self-esteem. Record the event you will focus on for this exercise below.

    _____

    _____

    _____

2. Now take a deep breath in and out.

3. Begin your bilateral stimulation and continue with it as you bring to mind the disruptive experience that you selected. Allow your mind to envision whatever comes up while continuing your bilateral stimulation for 30–60 seconds. Just notice whatever stands out.

4. After 30–60 seconds, whatever amount feels right to you, stop your bilateral stimulation and take in a big deep breath.

5. What details did you notice or have come to mind? For example, perhaps you noticed certain thoughts, vivid scenes or imagery, or sensations in your body. Whatever came to mind is important for you.

    _____

    _____

    _____

    _____

    _____

6. As you continue with this exercise, take a moment and bring to mind the calm place you imagined in chapter one.

7. As you envision your calm place, take a deep breath in and out. Once again start your bilateral stimulation and continue with this for about 30–60 seconds. Think about and notice all the sensations associated with your calm place. Focus on all the sensory details of this place (e.g., the smells, sounds, colors, physical sensations).

8. After about 30–60 seconds, whatever amount feels right for you, take a deep breath in and out, stopping your bilateral stimulation.

9. Take a moment and reflect on the differences you noticed between the sensations and thoughts of your calm place that you just envisioned and the sensations of the disruptive memory from the sequence before. How were they different? What stands out?

_____

_____

_____

_____

_____

10. Now, take a moment and do a scan of your bodily sensations, noticing any tension or anxiety that may have arisen anywhere in your body during this exercise. Notice where you store or harbor this within your body. Write down what you sense in your body.

_____

_____

_____

_____

_____

Tuning in to your body and mind will help you begin to identify physical sensations of discomfort that arise and may be triggering you to react. The more you can tune in to your body and mind, the more you can learn to identify what is causing these sensations. This exercise can assist you with learning more about yourself, teaching your mind to shift from being disrupted to calm, and managing your emotions.

Once you gain insight into how behaviors and patterns in your life have been useful, you can move to learning ways to calm this innate subconscious response to your triggers. Remove the judgment and allow yourself the freedom to objectively explore the reactions you have become accustomed to. Be aware that as you learn new information and adapt to new coping mechanisms, it takes your brain an average of thirty days to update and create this information as part of its normal processing.

Understanding Your Personal Triggers

As we discussed earlier, when you have experienced trauma, your brain reacts by trying to protect you from danger in the future. For example, if you were in a frightening car accident, your brain may remember the sound of the screeching tires or shattering glass, the smell of burning rubber or oil, and so on. Subsequently, if you hear screeching tires or smell burning rubber, your brain may think it is once again in danger because it saved these sensory details from the car accident as things that lead to danger. These sensations and triggers will act as your internal warning system in an effort to protect you.

Try to identify five of your own triggers, things that have a tendency to set you off. These are typically things that cause you to react or respond in a way you wouldn't normally. Write down all the triggers you can think of now.

1. _____

2. _____

3. _____

4. _____

5. _____

Now, think about what each of these personal triggers reminds you of. Does someone's tone of voice, or feeling pressure, or seeing or hearing something remind you of something unwanted from your past? Write down the memory that each trigger evokes.

Trigger	Evoked Memory
Example: People talking to you in a harsh or critical tone	*Example:* Being yelled at constantly by an abusive ex-partner

For each of your triggers, consider your typical behavioral or emotional response. For example, is it panic, anger, or silence? Do negative thoughts rush in and shower your mind? Or does your mind feel numb and empty? Write down your responses to your five triggers.

Trigger	Behavioral or Emotional Response

Now, look deeper to identify the beliefs that you arrive at when triggered.

Trigger	Corresponding belief about yourself or others

Do you judge yourself for acting or responding the way you do? If so, describe the judgment and how it affects you physically and emotionally.

_____

_____

_____

Where did you learn to judge yourself in this way?

_____

_____

_____

What keeps this response reoccurring? Does it feel stuck or out of your control?

_____

_____

_____

It may be easy for you to judge and criticize yourself and feel a sense of responsibility for some of your responses and reactions. But remember that your responses have served a purpose in the past, and honor them. They have in fact helped you be aware of danger, protected you, and perhaps ensured that more trauma would not occur.

These responses do not define who you are as a person. They are not personality traits; they are gut reactions hardwired to help you stay safe. When you begin to honor the responses you have, even when they appear negative, you allow room for change. Stop asking yourself "why" you do the things you do, and replace your internal dialogue with "how has this helped me?"

Slowing Your Responses to Triggers on the Spot

Triggers will always come and, as you know, can come out of nowhere at any time, unexpectedly. But you can begin to recognize and slow your response to triggers as they arise. You have done a lot of work thus far in this book that has prepared you to more insightfully identify your own triggers and responses. I hope that you will revisit the exercises throughout this workbook continually as you work with your own triggers and slowing your own response to these triggers.

A key skill for slowing down your reaction to triggers is acknowledging your responses as they arise and curiously observing where and what is occurring in your body and brain. This next exercise will help you learn to more efficiently manage your knee-jerk reactions by asking yourself certain questions. This form of exploration will be helpful as you continue learning how to handle triggers you may encounter.

Consider an event that occurred within the past week that annoyed, irritated, or upset you. Pick just a minor disturbance for this exercise so that you can practice becoming familiar with asking yourself these following questions.

My minor triggering experience: _____

Consider that this event or scenario is happening now, and ask yourself the following questions:

1. What is happening that you are responding to?

   _____

   _____

   _____

   _____

2. What are you being reminded of?

   _____

   _____

   _____

   _____

3. What you are noticing around you with your senses (sight, sound, smell, taste, touch)?

_____

_____

_____

4. What would happen if you waited to react to this? (Slowing your instinct to react gives you space to tune in to yourself.)

_____

_____

_____

5. What is one strength you have within you that can help you proceed?

_____

_____

_____

6. How have you responded previously to this trigger?

_____

_____

_____

7. How do you want to respond in this moment?

_____

_____

_____

8. Before responding, take seven deep breaths to help reset your nervous system. What happens when you do this?

_____

_____

_____

Practice walking through these questions in the moment, or as soon as you recognize a trigger occurring, to help you learn to slow your response. I would challenge you to consider using these questions as frequently as you can over the next week. The more you practice this process, the easier it will be for you to get to the solution and outcome that you are hoping to obtain.

When you face stressors or triggers, it is easy to become lost in the moment and overwhelmed by feelings, emotions, or circumstances. It is easy to forget just how far you have come and how close you actually are to the life you envision.

Draw on Your Strengths

Now that you have explored your trauma symptoms, personal triggers, and responses, we will turn to an exercise that will help you move past these symptoms and reactions by drawing on some of your strengths and enduring qualities. You can also find an audio recording of this exercise at http://www.newharbinger.com/49586.

I would like you to take a moment and reflect back on yourself throughout your lifetime. Specifically, recall a specific time when negative beliefs about yourself began to take hold. If you're having trouble picking a specific time in your past, try to think back to when you first noticed yourself becoming more reactive or doubting yourself.

Select the type of bilateral stimulation that you will be using for this exercise: eye movements, butterfly hug, knee tapping, or auditory stimulation. Remember to choose whichever bilateral stimulation method works for you and makes you feel comfortable. I will tell you when to add the bilateral stimulation and when to stop using it. When I prompt you to use the bilateral stimulation, you will do it for approximately 30–60 seconds.

To begin:

1. Find a comfortable, quiet place and position.

2. Take a moment and reflect back on yourself as a younger person. Bring to mind a specific time (or age) when you began to have negative beliefs about yourself or were confused by circumstances or people in your life. If you're having trouble picking a specific time in your

past, try to just bring to mind yourself as a child. Note below the specific age and/or description of your childhood self.

_____

_____

_____

_____

3. Now take a deep breath in and out.

4. Begin your bilateral stimulation and continue for the next 30–60 seconds with it as you envision yourself as a child from the image that you imagined above. As you continue with your bilateral stimulation, just take note of all that you notice as you begin with thinking of this child version of yourself.

    • What was this child fearful of? _____

    _____

    _____

    • How do you envision this child? _____

    _____

    _____

    Continuing your bilateral stimulation for 30–60 seconds. Just notice whatever stands out.

5. After 30–60 seconds, whatever amount feels right to you, stop your bilateral stimulation and take a big deep breath in and out.

6. What details did you notice or have come to mind?

    • Thoughts: _____

    _____

    _____

- Imagery: _____

  _____

  _____

- Sensations in your body: _____

  _____

  _____

- Write anything else that came to mind: _____

  _____

  _____

7. Take another deep breath in and out. Begin your bilateral stimulation again, continuing for approximately 30–60 seconds. As you continue with your bilateral stimulation, imagine your current self now. Notice the differences and/or similarities between yourself now and your child self you imagined before as you continue with your bilateral stimulation.

8. After 30–60 seconds, whatever specific amount feels right to you, stop your bilateral stimulation and take a big deep breath in and out.

   - What did you notice or have come to mind? _____

     _____

     _____

   - Were there certain differences between yourself then and now? _____

     _____

     _____

   - Was it an image of just your child self, just your adult self, or both? _____

     _____

     _____

- Write anything else that came to mind: _____

_____

_____

9. Taking a deep breath in and out, begin your bilateral stimulation again and bring to mind the image of yourself as a child and the image of yourself now. As you continue with your bilateral stimulation for 30–60 seconds, imagine that yourself now gets to go back in time and meet with this child version of yourself. Imagine how the child version of you would respond or interact with yourself now. Just notice—whatever comes to mind is right for you. Continue your bilateral stimulation for 30–60 seconds as you hold this image.

10. After 30–60 seconds, whatever specific amount feels right to you, stop your bilateral stimulation and take a big deep breath in and out.

11. What did you notice or have come to mind? For example, did your child self or self now say anything, or did one of them not want to interact with the other? Whatever came to mind is important for you. Feel free to note it below.

_____

_____

_____

_____

_____

_____

12. Take a breath in and out and add your bilateral stimulation again for approximately 30–60 seconds. As you continue with your bilateral stimulation, bring up this child version of yourself and your self now again, meeting together. Is there anything the child would like to say to your current adult self? Is there anything that your self now would like to say to the child? How do they each respond? What do they need from each other? Is there anything that this child self would need to feel safe with this current version of you? Continue your bilateral stimulation for 30–60 seconds, noticing whatever comes to mind.

Take a deep breath in and out, stopping your bilateral stimulation.

- What did your child self say? _____

_____

_____

- What did your adult self now say? _____

_____

_____

- How did they respond to one another? Did they listen, ignore, or ask questions? _____

_____

_____

- Why do you think that was the response? _____

_____

_____

- What do you feel they both needed from each other? For example, did they need to be heard, to be noticed, to know they are safe?

_____

_____

_____

13. Take a breath in and out and add your bilateral stimulation for about 30–60 seconds, as you continue to notice the interaction between your child self and current self. Imagine your current self as you show your child self all the skills, abilities, and knowledge you have learned throughout the years. Let this child version of you know how far you have come, as you continue your bilateral stimulation for 30–60 seconds.

14. Breathe deeply in and out while stopping your bilateral stimulation. What things did you say or show your child self that you are able to do or know?

_____

_____

_____

15. Breathe in and out, starting your bilateral stimulation once more. As you do, imagine yourself inviting your child self to come along with you now in your life as you continue to learn and grow. Let this child know that you are bigger, stronger, and smarter now and will protect them. Thank your child self for helping you the way they have throughout all the years. Hold this image in your mind as you continue your bilateral stimulation for approximately 60 seconds.

16. On this last set, as you breathe in and out, slowly start your bilateral stimulation again, this time just noticing how the child version of you is safe. This child version of you is now protected by your current self and doesn't have to work so hard to keep you safe. Continue your bilateral stimulation for approximately 30 seconds as you embrace this image. Give this image compassion, support, and grace.

17. Take a deep breath in, stop your bilateral stimulation, and reflect on what you want to remember from this exercise.

_____

_____

_____

_____

_____

_____

_____

_____

You have just completed a great deal of inner work. Congratulate yourself and reflect back on what stood out for you during this exercise. By doing this internal work, you not only learn to develop empathy and compassion for your younger self but also begin to shift your brain into the present moment, where you are more able to recognize your strengths and abilities. You can use this exercise at times when you feel stuck, triggered, or anxious.

You have done a lot of personal growth throughout this chapter. You have learned about the root causes of your trauma symptoms and PTSD, the way your brain and body are linked together, and important resources and skills that you can use to shift your perspective and calm the lingering symptoms you experience. We often forget just how far we have come in our journey. I hope this chapter gave you insight and awareness that will help you spring forward into the life you are working so hard to create.

CHAPTER SEVEN

Heal in the Present Moment

Whatever the present moment contains, accept it as if you had chosen it. Always work with it, not against it.

—Eckhart Tolle

Jadyn was a devoted and loving spouse who had spent nine years dealing with his wife's addiction. He had entered his marriage naïve to the intensity and destruction that the disease of alcoholism could cause, unaware of the heartache and trauma that would soon engulf him and rob him of his dreams.

A few years into their marriage, Jadyn began to notice that Betty's drinking had slowly been escalating to the point of concern and confronted Betty on these issues. She acknowledged that her drinking had in fact gotten out of hand and agreed to cut back. As life moved forward, Betty and Jadyn agreed to begin starting their own family. Months of effort for Betty to become pregnant resulted in failed attempts, and they sought out medical assistance to gain answers. They were devastated to learn that they had a low probability of ever conceiving on their own. Shortly afterward, Betty learned that she was pregnant, against the odds. Shocked but grateful, they began to prepare for this miracle they had been given. A few months into the pregnancy, however, Betty had a miscarriage.

Shattered, Betty tried to remain hopeful about the possibility of somehow getting to start a family with Jadyn. However, over time, the loss seemed to destroy her. Her drinking once again began to escalate; lying, anger, and abusive behavior ensued, and soon alcoholism had fully taken over. In denial of her addiction, Betty continued to spiral out of control. Jadyn found countless hidden bottles of whiskey and unaccounted-for prescriptions. Desperate to save their marriage and help the person he loved most, Jadyn learned as much as he could about addiction and attempted any avenue possible to get Betty help. Multiple hospitalizations and warnings from countless doctors about the potential of her liver and kidneys shutting down seemed to have no effect. Realizing that the addiction seemed to have won, Jadyn eventually filed for divorce. Betty remained checked out and avoidant, strung out in her addictive pattern, and Jadyn was left with facing the aftermath of trauma from their tumultuous marriage and Betty's abusive behavior. He felt panic and fear of doing something wrong, even long after Betty was no longer around to blame him for her struggles. His struggles with anger, confusion, despair, and regret kept him as a prisoner to his past.

Close to a year after separating and waiting for Betty to respond to the divorce paperwork, Jadyn learned that Betty had been admitted to the hospital after her liver and kidneys shut down from her abuse of alcohol. For close to a month she remained in the hospital, the doctors feeling it would be touch-and-go based on the damage that had already been done. Upon learning this news, Jadyn had a choice to make. He could allow his past to control his responses and avoid the inevitable, or he could choose to do what he felt was right for himself in the present moment. Being the graceful, forgiving, loving man that he is, Jadyn extended help to Betty and this time she accepted. She was discharged from the hospital and given strict instructions to not drink for the few days before she would be taken to inpatient treatment for her alcoholism. Jadyn cared for her over these few days, but Betty's condition suddenly declined and she was taken back to the hospital. Jadyn learned that she had drunk, and the doctor discharged her to hospice care, explaining that this last drinking bout had destroyed her liver and kidneys fully. Too weak to fully understand what was taking place, Betty was sent to her grandparents' home, Jadyn by her side. He stayed there and loved her, even expressing forgiveness and sorrow for the pain that she must have endured. A few weeks later, Betty passed away.

Jadyn shared that he made the choice to show up for Betty when she began to decline based on his own intuition, insisting that this would somehow help him heal and give him the closure that he had been unable to get. He had every reason to remain distanced and absent and let the anger and pain of Betty's abuse keep him numb and closed off. However, he knew that there was no distance he could go that would drown out the symptoms he still faced from their traumatic marriage. He finally learned to trust himself and do what was right for him in the moment—not what the past would say was right or what the future may anticipate. He chose to be present among the pain and to show up in her time of death as an effort to heal his own wounds, more than even hers.

As time has passed for Jadyn, he shared that learning to show up for himself and what he needs in the present moment has proven to be the most helpful. He reminded me that as a result of suffering from PTSD, you rarely turn to what you think you need. You become conditioned to believe that everyone else has the answers and that you cannot choose what is best for yourself. The truth, in fact, is that you are the expert of your own life. You hold all your own answers and are capable of finding your own solutions within yourself if you choose to do so. I hope you will make the commitment, like Jadyn, to stay in the present and do what is right for you, when you need it. Honor yourself in the here and now.

In this chapter, you are going to learn how to stay grounded and present in your current life. You will learn skills to assist you as you break free from the chains of your past and expand your compassion toward the wounded parts of yourself that still require time and attention to truly heal. I will also help you get to know each of your own feelings and emotions—which you can consider as "parts" of your mind—in order for you to stay present when they arise at unwanted times.

Identifying Your Internal Parts

The different emotional parts of your mind are meant to be harmonious, meaning that they are intended to work together. I recommend that you watch the Disney movie *Inside Out*, which follows the inner workings of feelings and emotions that occur within the main character and how her feelings and emotions develop, respond, and interact with one another. Throughout this film, you are shown how all of your own feelings are meant to come together and assist one another. When this occurs, you are able to experience things the way they were intended to be experienced. For example, maybe you have had a very disappointing experience in a close relationship with someone in which you were let down or hurt. As painful as this experience was, perhaps it has allowed you to more fully appreciate efforts of love, support, and acceptance from other close relationships, as you know what it is like to not have these things.

Part of what will assist in your own healing journey and allow you to stay in the present moment is learning how to recreate harmony within yourself and toward your own dynamic feelings and emotions. As a trauma survivor, you know that it is easy to judge yourself or despise certain emotions you may have from time to time. All of your experiences can become opportunities for growth and expansion. You will find that it is natural and okay to experience a variety of emotions and that you have the freedom to explore these emotions and learn what to do with them as they arise.

You learned in chapter six how these parts of your mind, these responses, were formed as a means of survival. In addition, some of your mindscape was created with the expectations, roles, and values placed on you as a child. As you aged, you inherently took on some of these same emotions and feelings from your own environment and learned how to function with these feelings and emotions. In order for you to learn how to stay present in the here and now and manage triggers as they arise, you will need to learn how to welcome and identify the different parts associated with your feelings. This will require you to feel some of the discomfort and to begin to tune in to your intuitive "gut" response, as Jadyn did in the opening story.

You may have felt that it was unsafe to explore your feelings and emotions in the past; this is typically the case for people who have experienced trauma. It is common to feel somewhat detached and far away from the unique characteristics that make you *you*. But these very things—those that are specific and individual to you—are beautiful and important. The world needs what you have to offer. Let's begin this process by safely tuning in to your inner world.

Get to Know Your Inner World

This exercise will open you up to being in close proximity with your mind, body, and soul. This is a grounding exercise, one that can help you learn to recenter yourself by consciously listening and attuning to your inner world. This will challenge you to go inside and observe the inner workings of your mind. It may be helpful to listen to the audio recording of this exercise, available at http://www.newharbinger.com/49586.

Select the type of bilateral stimulation that you will be using for this exercise: eye movements, butterfly hug, knee tapping, or auditory stimulation. Remember to choose whichever bilateral stimulation method works for you and makes you feel comfortable. I will tell you when to add the bilateral stimulation and when to stop using it. When I prompt you to use the bilateral stimulation, you will do it for approximately 30–60 seconds.

To begin:

1. Find a comfortable, quiet place and position.

2. Now, close your eyes and take a moment to just be present with yourself. Notice your particular thoughts, feelings, emotions, and even the sensations within your body. Just listen and observe as you tune in to your inner world. After about 30 seconds, open your eyes.

    What did you notice? _____

    _____

3. This time, as you take a deep breath in and out, begin your bilateral stimulation and continue with it as you begin to listen and observe the inner parts of your mind. What thoughts, feelings, sensations, or even images stand out the most to you? Continue to ponder this for about 30–60 seconds, then stop your bilateral stimulation.

4. Take a deep breath in and out. Write down what arose in your inner world.

    Thoughts: _____

    _____

    _____

Feelings: _____

_____

_____

Sensations: _____

_____

_____

Images: _____

_____

_____

What stood out most to me was: _____

_____

_____

5. Allow yourself another deep breath in and out, begin your bilateral stimulation, and call to mind the element that stood out the most. What is this part trying to express? Is there something that this part of you needs? It might be to express itself, be listened to, share its needs, or offer you a message. Just notice. Continue with this imagery for 30–60 seconds.

6. Take a deep breath in and out, and stop your bilateral stimulation. Consider the following:

What did this part of you express? _____

_____

_____

What, if anything, does this part of you need? _____

_____

If this part had a message for you, what would it be? _____

_____

_____

7. Breathe in and out, and again add your bilateral stimulation while you bring up the part of you that most wants your attention today. Recall whatever was expressed, identified, or needed that you just noticed. Continuing with your bilateral stimulation, ask, *What would help me understand this part more?* Just observe the insight or realizations that occur as you listen, acknowledge, and recognize this part of yourself. Notice what comes to your mind as you continue for 30–60 seconds.

8. Take a deep breath in and out, stopping your bilateral stimulation. Write down the following:

    Any insights or realizations that arose as you explored this: _____

    _____

    _____

    Anything you need to do to help you understand this part of yourself more: _____

    _____

    _____

    Any feelings you need to acknowledge to support this part of yourself more: _____

    _____

    _____

9. Breathe in and out, adding your bilateral stimulation for another 30–60 seconds as you simply notice and recognize the needs, thoughts, or insights that you are discovering as you move through this self-exploration exercise. As you do this, notice if there is anything positive that you would like to tell or remind yourself. Continue your bilateral stimulation for 30–60 seconds as you reflect on this.

10. Stop your bilateral stimulation, taking a deep breath in and out.

    What compassionate or positive things did you tell yourself? _____

    _____

    _____

11. Begin your bilateral stimulation once more, drawing a deep breath in and out. As you continue with your bilateral stimulation, encourage this part of yourself by reminding yourself that you are working on healing—that you are committed to becoming the best version of you, even if that takes time. Offer yourself thanks for being brave enough and strong enough to continue moving forward as you have for as long as you have.

12. After 30–60 seconds, stop your bilateral stimulation and release a big breath out.

    What did you say to encourage this part of yourself? _____

    _____

    _____

    What did you give thanks or gratitude for to this part of you? _____

    _____

    _____

13. Close your eyes for a moment and notice how it feels to lean into yourself and deeply listen as you have been doing. What creativity and vastness exist within yourself and your mind? Take as long as you need to envision this strongly. Then draw this vision.

14. Breathe in and out slowly, taking notice of how your body feels. Scan your body from top to bottom and see if there is anywhere that you are holding any type of disturbance or tension.

15. As you continue to take deep breaths, imagine sending relaxation and peace to any of these physical places that are carrying stress. If you feel like adding bilateral stimulation to this part of the exercise you can, keeping your bilateral stimulation to 30 seconds. But again, only if you choose.

16. Once you feel relaxed, take a moment and notice how you are continuing to grow and learning to free yourself as you move forward on your healing journey.

As you begin to learn to listen to yourself, becoming curious about the inner workings of your mind, your body, and your own needs, you are likely beginning to have more compassion for yourself. This newfound self-compassion will assist you as you learn to bring a new sense of appreciation and love for all the diverse parts of yourself.

To soften some of the protective roles and behaviors that you have adapted to, start becoming curious about the parts of yourself that seem rigid, that you don't want, or that you judge. For example, maybe you hate that you lose your temper occasionally and that you explode with anger and say hurtful things when you are triggered. But if you were to get curious and explore this emotion, you might learn that it is not trying to harm you. Maybe when you reflect on your own exploding temper, you find that this behavior was the example used in your home growing up, or perhaps the only time that you feel heard or taken seriously has been when you have reached a breaking point and reacted with anger. When you shift to using curiosity regarding these unwanted, shameful parts or reactions you hold, you will begin to identify why and how they formed.

As you become more familiar with these reactions and acknowledge why they became a habit for you, you will slowly begin to have compassion for yourself, and you will be able to see these as past responses that were carried with you into the present moment, rather than a present choice that you are consciously making. You will also learn alternative ways to express your needs and emotions.

Acknowledging Diversity Within Yourself

Learning about yourself in this way for the first time is a challenge but also brings relief. Some of the resistant or most critical parts of you have likely been developed through watching, learning, and mimicking people from earlier in your life. Usually the parts (reactions, behaviors, and so on) of yourself that you don't like or are ashamed of have been rejected by others that you have encountered in your life. These distinct characteristics of yourself are usually parts of your personality that you don't trust or that feel the most vulnerable. The more you understand all these inner workings of your mind, the more likely you will be to navigate and free yourself from the shame and judgment you hold about yourself. You will come to learn that all of your reactions, responses, emotions, and behaviors have had important roles and functions within your life.

When you begin to offer the critical, misunderstood parts of yourself compassion, they will soften and you may learn that the critical parts of yourself are more based on fears of your past experiences that you are trying to protect yourself from. If you can use the previous exercise for aspects of your personality that you don't fully understand, you will learn a lot about yourself and your responses. You will be able to give yourself some space to acknowledge the responsibility that much of you has had to carry throughout the years.

Now is the time to explore how you want to engage and respond. You get to discover all your own possibilities that have been restricted that no longer have to stay this way. Remember that sometimes change is hard to identify, and you may misinterpret difficult emotions as setbacks. Sparks of change can take on many forms and can include your ability to acknowledge your pain. Allow yourself time to grieve, feel, or befriend parts of yourself that have been neglected. Showing this care, kindness, and a softening in your attitude toward yourself will build your confidence.

Caring for the Wounded Aspects Within

When you experience traumatic, painful things in life, it is easy to deny, push away from, or bury these vulnerable pieces of yourself because of how deeply they have been wounded. You will not be able to fully heal if you keep parts of yourself restricted or abandoned. As we continue forward in this book together, you will continue to learn just how essential it is for you to form a secure attachment with yourself. Using curiosity and exploring all the different aspects of yourself and your reactions lead to developing this type of intimate attachment with all parts of yourself, the good and the bad. Imagine looking toward yourself just as if you were looking toward a young child. When you begin to use empathy and become more inquisitive toward these wounded parts of yourself, you can begin to restore and heal them.

I want to help you learn how to get back to the core of who you are and retrieve these unique distinguishing factors. This process is almost like a computer update that will help you stay in the here and now and function more effectively, just as a software update allows a system to operate and run more smoothly. As you begin to show the repressed and/or shamed parts of yourself all the potential, strength, and growth that you have achieved, you will find that these parts have been critical in shaping you. This process will start to reveal the clarity needed to release and forgive yourself, and compassionately embrace the pain you have endured, becoming truly unburdened and freed.

As you do this, consider asking yourself about what strengths each of your rejected or shamed attributes of yourself actually holds. This is an act of empowerment. Empowerment is the process of becoming stronger or more confident and claiming your rights. Empowerment is taking control back of your own life. Empowerment comes from within and comes from accepting all of what has made you who you are, even the difficult parts of yourself. As you get ready to begin the next exercise, you will get a clear look at just how this is done. These rejected, shamed pieces of yourself likely need a break and reprieve from the heaviness that they have carried. This activity will assist you in being able to "unburden" this pain.

Free Your Wounded Parts

This exercise will assist you with updating and freeing your repressed parts. Many of the parts of yourself that you end up abandoning or hiding have been hurt and have never had the freedom to express themselves. I recommend that you practice this exercise anytime you feel the need to acknowledge or free a part of yourself that has been repressed. Have a place in mind—such as your calm place from chapter one—that can offer a sense of retreat should you need temporary relief from your pain. It may be helpful for you to read through this exercise a few times until you are familiar with the steps and can do it easily from memory. You can also download an audio recording of the exercise at http://www.newharbinger.com/49586.

Select the type of bilateral stimulation that you will be using for this exercise: eye movements, butterfly hug, knee tapping, or auditory stimulation. Remember to choose whichever bilateral stimulation method works for you and makes you feel comfortable. I will tell you when to add the bilateral stimulation and when to stop using it. When I prompt you to use the bilateral stimulation, you will do it for approximately 30–60 seconds.

1. Start by bringing up your calm place from chapter one. Remember that this is a calming, relaxing place that you have visited, or wish to revisit, or it can be a place you haven't been. It can be completely imaginative, as well. This should be a place that represents peace, tranquility, and joy.

2. Find a comfortable, quiet place and position.

3. Now, close your eyes and take a deep breath in and out as you begin your bilateral stimulation. Bring to mind your calm place for about 30 seconds.

4. Breathing in and out, open your eyes.

What place did you notice? _____

_____

5. Take a deep breath in and out and continue with the bilateral stimulation as you focus on the image of the place for the next 30–60 seconds.

6. Stop your bilateral stimulation and note each of the following: (It may be helpful to make notes to help you connect with the sensations of this place in the future.)

    Sight: What do you see in this place—the colors, time of day, sights, if anyone is with you or if you are alone? _____

    _____

    _____

    Smell: What does it smell like in this place? _____

    _____

    _____

    Hearing: What sounds are you experiencing in this place? Is it quiet, soft, loud, soothing; is there music or talking? _____

    _____

    _____

    Taste: Are you eating or drinking anything in this place? _____

    _____

    _____

    Touch/Physical: What are you doing in this place? Are you sitting, standing, being still or active? Notice how you feel physically in this place. Notice the temperature of this place, if it is warm or cold. Notice how you feel emotionally in this place. _____

    _____

    _____

7. As you take a deep breath in and out, begin your bilateral stimulation again and bring to mind or identify a part of yourself that seems wounded and needs relief. For example, this could be an anxious, sad, or angry part of yourself. It could be a younger version of yourself. After about 30–60 seconds, stop your bilateral stimulation and breathe in and out.

    What part, or aspect, of yourself came to mind as needing some relief? _____

    _____

    _____

    _____

8. Begin your bilateral stimulation, continuing as you envision this aspect, emotion, or part of yourself. Imagine taking this part of you and guiding it to your calm place, where you can allow it to rest and be free from carrying such a heavy burden. Continue your bilateral stimulation for about 60 seconds or as long as you need to fully envision this.

9. Stop your bilateral stimulation and take a deep breath in and out.

    Describe what you felt as you envisioned your burdened part in a calm place. _____

    _____

    _____

    If you feel a sense of relief, describe it. _____

    _____

    _____

    If you were unable to fully envision getting to the calm place and finding some relaxation, you may want to go back and repeat step 9 until you find relief.

10. After you are able to envision finding some relief, begin your bilateral stimulation once more, continuing as you bring to mind this wounded part of yourself, safely within your calm place. Offer the wounded part of yourself some assurance, saying, *It is okay for you to rest. It is okay for you to relieve yourself from the heaviness of* _____ (responsibility, fear, shame, or whatever pain it is holding). Allow this part of you to embrace this calm place, where it

can breathe and be free. After 30–60 seconds, discontinue your bilateral stimulation and take a deep breath in and out.

How did this feel? _____

_____

_____

Did you find relief? If so, what relief did you experience? _____

_____

_____

11. Close your eyes, and just allow your whole self to know that you are safe now. You never have to return to the painful places you have been before and can visit or revisit this image of your calm place with any of the parts of yourself that need relief as frequently as you need to.

12. Taking a final breath in and out, start your bilateral stimulation, and continue with it as you imagine taking the calmness and other feelings of this place and spreading it throughout your entire body. After about 30–60 seconds, or when you feel at peace, stop your bilateral stimulation.

Take a moment to reflect on any discoveries or realizations that you had from offering yourself freedom and relief within your own calm place.

_____

_____

_____

_____

_____

_____

_____

How has this exercise been useful to you? What hope does it inspire?

_____

_____

_____

_____

_____

I hope you experienced a sense of freedom. Notice the freedom and breathe it in. Notice the way that you were able to escape some of the bondage from your past experiences and envision these wounded parts of yourself free at last. You are teaching yourself to thrive, not just survive. You are discovering that you are resilient.

As you continue to unburden yourself and build on this sense of calm, you will find that this aids in your overall sense of resiliency. I want you to revisit your three statements from chapter five that account for deepening your spirit of resiliency and that will continue to assist you in unburdening yourself. These statements include "I have…," "I am…," and "I can…." You can repeat the statements you already created, or you can come up with new ones.

- Acknowledge the resources you have available by saying: *I have* _____

_____

_____

- Give yourself value by saying: *I am* _____

_____

_____

- Show hope for the future by saying: *I can* _____

_____

_____

Embrace these statements of resiliency and use them in your healing work. You are uncovering all that has always been within you, and these statements will motivate you to keep going.

As we come to the close of this chapter, I want to leave you with an exercise that I believe you will find uplifting and encouraging.

The Path You're Walking

This exercise will help put your life, experiences, growth, and progress into a perspective that will fill you with hope and confidence that you can, in fact, arrive at your desired place in life. To download an audio recording of this exercise, please go to http://www.newharbinger.com/49586.

Select the type of bilateral stimulation that you will be using for this exercise: eye movements, butterfly hug, knee tapping, or auditory stimulation. Remember to choose whichever bilateral stimulation method works for you and makes you feel comfortable. I will tell you when to add the bilateral stimulation and when to stop using it. When I prompt you to use the bilateral stimulation, you will do it for approximately 30–60 seconds.

I want you to envision a path; it can be any path or trail—somewhere that you have or haven't been, real or imagined. The destination may still seem somewhat unclear, but just notice yourself standing at the base of this path.

1. As you imagine this path, take a deep breath in and out and begin your bilateral stimulation, continuing as you envision all the sights and sounds that surround you. Notice the scenery, colors, temperature, and all the elements of your path. As you stand at the foot of this path, imagine looking ahead, into somewhat unfamiliar territory. What do you anticipate as you look ahead? Continue for approximately 30–60 seconds.

2. Take a deep breath in and out, stopping your bilateral stimulation. Record what you observed about this path.

   • Scenery: _____

   _____

   • Colors: _____

   _____

   • Temperature: _____

   _____

   • Elements of nature present: _____

   _____

3. Breathing in and out, begin your bilateral stimulation again and continue with it as you imagine this path once again. This time as you look ahead, envision that the path leads to something you have always desired to do, go to, or experience. Essentially, what would you like there to be at the end of this path, waiting for you? After 30–60 seconds, stop your bilateral stimulation.

    What did you imagine lying at the end of this path? _____

    _____

    _____

4. As you envision this path and the positive image or place that lies at the final destination, begin your bilateral stimulation again, and this time imagine looking back toward the path that led to this final destination. Consider all you have overcome to get to this ultimate place. Notice all the obstacles you have faced and just how far you have come as you stand in this place of true healing. After 30–60 seconds, stop your bilateral stimulation.

    • What did you notice as you looked back on the path from this destination?

      _____

      _____

      _____

    • What helped you arrive at this final landing? _____

      _____

      _____

5. Add your bilateral stimulation once more. As you consider the end landing place of your path and your current circumstances, how close to healing do you actually feel? Stop your bilateral stimulation after 30–60 seconds.

    • Where did you see yourself on the path in relation to the final destination? Were you close or far away?

      _____

      _____

      _____

- In relation to the entirety of the path, just how far have you come since the beginning of this journey?

_____

_____

_____

6. Take a deep breath in and out and start your bilateral stimulation. Notice again just how far you have come on this path. As you do, look ahead to the final destination, and notice the hope that is waiting for you and just how close you actually are to arriving. After 30–60 seconds, stop your bilateral stimulation.

- What gave you hope as you looked ahead? _____

_____

_____

- What do you want to hold on to or remember from this exercise that will help you remember just how far you have actually come?

_____

_____

_____

I hope you realize that the end of your path is reachable and attainable. You have come so far, more than you recognize at times. Acknowledge the obstacles you have already overcome and the strength you carry that keeps you moving forward. Keep holding on to this vision of what awaits you; you are getting closer.

CHAPTER EIGHT

Unlock Your Future

The secret of change is to focus all of your energy, not on fighting the old, but on building the new.

—Dan Millman

If you would have told me years ago that someday I would write a book on trauma, PTSD, and EMDR, I would not have believed you. The messages that I have received throughout most of my life have probably been similar to some of the messages that you have received. These were messages that I believed for decades because I had rarely heard anything different, some of which weren't embedded until I was an adult. These messages ranged from being crazy, broken, unstable, impulsive, and incapable of change. I have spent a lot of years trying to challenge and prove these messages wrong, hoping that if I could somehow change the minds of these people and the voices that formed these opinions, I could be free. I slowly learned that the freedom did not lie within the opinions and acceptance of others but truly only existed within myself.

I wish I could tell you that healing and choosing this path is easy, but it's not. It is challenging and at times feels endless. There will be obstacles and points in your journey where you want to give up and doubt your endurance and ability to keep going. I have been there time and time again and there is one thing that has kept me going: I am not a quitter and neither are you.

I am deeply rooted in being a survivor. My pain has taught me to endure hardship. It has taught me resiliency to keep going even when I don't want to. It has taught me to be a fighter and push through, even when all the odds are against me. Somewhere, I came to learn that all the pain, trauma, and heartache I have faced are responsible for some of my greatest gifts, just as they surely are for you. I have come to accept that I cannot change anything from my past; as much as I have tried to avoid, ignore, and change it, it is impossible. I wonder if you have found or are finding what I have found—that my past has led me to humility. The lack of love ironically taught me to love with my whole heart. The abuse and pain taught me to be a fighter and a warrior and claim my power again. It has taught me to see others who have been overlooked. You have all these same abilities and characteristics, even if you are facing different symptoms.

I hope, like me, you will stop fighting the battles of your past. Take that pain and trauma and use it to propel you into persevering and embracing your purpose. You can create, build, do, and be anything you wish to. Even if you do it afraid and trembling, you can do it because you are nothing short of a survivor.

Finding Your Purpose

The distinctiveness of your own experiences is the hallmark of what makes you uniquely gifted and talented. Among these unique capabilities also lies your purpose. Purpose symbolizes the reason for your existence. Finding your life's purpose is what will guide, influence, shape, mold, and direct you toward achieving your goals in life. Your purpose is usually rooted to the things you feel the most passionate about. Passion and purpose are intertwined and both serve as motivators for one another.

Often, the purpose you once dreamed of and envisioned becomes lost when you wrestle in the throes of trauma and/or PTSD. You may feel that your past experiences have permanently damaged your inner world and forever corrupted or changed the hopes and vision that you once held for yourself. What if I told you that the deepest of wounds have the ability to transform you and bring about qualities and traits that you never knew existed?

I like to use the analogy of refining gold. Gold is discovered in a relatively pure form. However, even in its purest form, gold is often too soft to be used by itself. As a result, other metals are frequently added to it in order to strengthen it. These other metals are often not as valuable and do not carry as much luster, but when combined with the gold, the result allows for solid endurance, leading to the gold's true intended purpose.

The purpose that you hold is gold. The intentions of your heart and soul are pure. The challenges that you endure can be used as additives, just like they are in the process of refining gold. They can increase your endurance, enhance your gifts, and make your life brighter and fuller. We all have the tendency to seek and continue with what is familiar and comfortable. However, if we stick with our familiarity, we may miss the opportunity to be transformed or become more than we realized.

Redefining Your Past

If you seek to find the moments from your past that you wish to redefine, you can remove the limits you once placed on yourself. You can take the difficult, treacherous mountains that you have faced and show yourself and others that you are equipped to overcome any limitation set in front of you.

As you do, you will also inspire and encourage those around you to take on and confront their own barriers. You were not created to stay stuck or be limited by your past. You were created to evolve and grow.

One way of intentionally redefining your past involves being selective in the battles you choose to fight. You will have to be mindful and refuse to give energy and time to areas of your life that do not need your attention. Focus on fighting for things that will lead to growth and potential and will set your soul on fire.

Melody Beattie, author of *Codependent No More*, discusses the importance of looking back on our past circumstances and seeing them as teachers. She encourages us to look at every circumstance as a lesson and teaching moment. If you take on this perspective, I wonder what lessons you will find from your own past. Consider what positive or helpful lessons you have learned throughout your toughest encounters. Taking this a step further, I would challenge you to consider:

What are your three best attributes or characteristics?

1. _____

2. _____

3. _____

How did each of these develop in spite of—and maybe even because of—the painful trauma you have endured?

Characteristic 1: _____

_____

_____

Characteristic 2: _____

_____

_____

Characteristic 3: _____

_____

_____

Your greatest victory will always come after your biggest struggles. Part of what makes this true is that struggle develops humility—if we allow it. A friend of mine who struggled with PTSD and addiction told me once that "the good never feels as good without the bad." There is so much raw honesty in this concept. Your appreciation and gratitude for things has the potential to be magnified if you can see your experiences as guideposts and not just hitching posts.

In order to master this skill, I want to introduce you to an exercise that will help you differentiate between what you feel and what you know, and will teach you the power of creating a life with intention.

In the table below, make a list of things that you are currently struggling with that elicit a great deal of distress, anxiety, or fear. Next, list the feelings associated with each stressor. Last, identify the facts of the situation and a personal strength or truth about yourself.

What I Feel, What I Know

Current Stressors	What You Feel	What You Know to Be True About Your Strengths
Example: not being in control at work	anxious, crazy, unorganized	I work hard and always give my best. I am getting stuff done that I need to do.

Use this exercise as needed when you find yourself facing challenges that you are uncertain you can overcome. Tune in to whatever strengths you can find, no matter how small, and you will begin to see your perspective and attitude change drastically.

What You Are Becoming

You have already gone into the darkest parts of your life and faced your fears. You have acquired more strength and value than you realize. The smallest steps in the right direction are planting the seeds of potential for all that you can achieve moving forward in your life. You can always learn to do better and be better; it just takes acknowledging your strengths, weaknesses, and inner barriers, and being persistent with practicing and using the exercises that you have learned. You may have not been able to write the beginning or other parts of your story, but you have the power and choice to write your own ending from this point forward. What do you want the narrative of your story to be?

Braving Your Future

To handle the fears about your future and prepare you with confidence, I want to leave you with one last exercise and experience of hope. If you wish, you can download an audio recording of this exercise at http://www.newharbinger.com/49586.

Bring to mind a future event that you are anxious or worried about or are facing with anticipation.

Future scenario: _____

As you consider this future scenario, which part feels the most intense or stands out the most?

_____

_____

_____

What negative belief about yourself or perceived fear do you have regarding this scenario?

_____

_____

_____

What positive belief would you like to have about yourself that would make this vision of the future feel more attainable?

_____

_____

_____

Notice the emotions that come up as you think about this future issue, and also notice any physical disturbance in your body and where it is occurring. Reflect on what you notice.

_____

_____

_____

Select the type of bilateral stimulation that you will be using for this exercise: eye movements, butterfly hug, knee tapping, or auditory stimulation. Remember to choose whichever bilateral stimulation method works for you and makes you feel comfortable. I will tell you when to add the bilateral stimulation and when to stop using it. When I prompt you to use the bilateral stimulation, you will do it for approximately 30–60 seconds.

1. Bring up the future fear or anxious anticipation you just identified. As you do, notice the worst part of this fear, along with the feelings and emotions surrounding this event.

2. Add your bilateral stimulation as you continue to think of this image of the future. After 30–60 seconds, take a deep breath in and out and stop your bilateral stimulation.

   What stood out as you envisioned this future scenario? _____

   _____

   _____

3. Taking a breath in and out, begin your bilateral stimulation and, as you do, notice what makes this future event feel uncomfortable or overwhelming. Continue for 30–60 seconds and then stop your bilateral stimulation.

What made this future event feel uncomfortable or overwhelming? _____

_____

_____

4. As you start your bilateral stimulation again, focus on these elements of the future that feel uncomfortable or overwhelming, but this time think of a positive belief that you would like to have regarding this situation. Continue for about 30–60 seconds.

   What was the positive belief that you identified? _____

   _____

   _____

5. Begin your bilateral stimulation and, as you do, notice what could assist you in relieving the tension or discomfort around this future situation. What would help you believe the positive belief that you identified regarding this situation? Stop your bilateral stimulation after 30–60 seconds.

   What did you identify that could assist you in relieving this tension or help you face this situation more confidently? _____

   _____

   _____

   _____

   _____

6. Begin your bilateral stimulation. Envision yourself in the future being able to face and successfully engage in the anticipated event. Notice yourself reacting, responding, and being present in this future moment the way you desire to be. Take 30–60 seconds or longer until you feel that you can fully envision yourself in this future scenario, then stop your bilateral stimulation.

What happened when you were able to bring your strengths to the future scenario?

_____

_____

_____

7. Take a deep breath in and out, begin your bilateral stimulation one last time and, as you do, hold the positive belief you wish to live out as the image of this future scenario. After 15–30 seconds, take a deep breath in and out, then stop your bilateral stimulation.

What positive belief did you witness happening? _____

_____

_____

How did the imagined scenario unfold? _____

_____

_____

8. Close your eyes and do a brief body scan from head to toe, noticing if any tension is still being held in your body. If it is, just breathe and imagine sending positive energy to those parts that still hold tension.

9. Take a moment and notice that you were able to envision yourself successfully overcoming this future scenario. Even if you had to repeat this exercise multiple times before you fully felt the effects, you still were able to change your perspective.

Feel free to use this exercise when you need it to work through future scenarios that cause you anxiety or stress. You are continuing to be brave and embracing your future.

Embracing Your True Identity and Resilience

As I leave you at this point in your journey, I want you to imagine that you get to create a new boat in which you can sail away. You are now the master of your sea. You get to embark on a journey of your own desire and direction, and where you are headed is surely miraculous and beyond anything you ever thought possible. As you sail on, know that the wreckage and waves from the past struggles of your life have helped you prepare for this new voyage and led you to constructing a new boat full of life rafts. This will allow you to overcome and successfully get past any wreckage or devastating obstacles that you may face. Your boat doesn't just ensure your own safety and survival, but has the potential to offer life rafts to other survivors just like you, trying to find their way out of the storm.

How will you choose to continue your journey? _____

_____

_____

_____

_____

Acknowledgments

First and foremost, this book would not have been possible without the ongoing trust, vulnerability, and patience provided by all the valiant clients that I have had the honor to serve. There could never be enough words of gratitude that could express the love, admiration, and respect I hold for each of you. Thank you for inspiring me and teaching me with your genuine, messy authenticity. You are the most brave, authentic examples of love and hope, never stopping being yourselves. This book was for each of you.

Alexis and Caryn—You both have been my anchor and beam of light in the storm. The endless shoulder rubs, listening to countless rereads, calming my self-doubt, and the daily battle of keeping me on task and focused is no small feat. You two have continued to encourage me and see me for who I truly am. I am truly blessed to have you on *our* team. I love you both like family. From the bottom of my heart, thank you.

PESI—Writing this almost brings me to tears. Anna Rustick, you took a chance on a crazy idea I had to start training and have never once questioned or doubted me. Ryan Bartholome, you almost feel like my agent and continue to give me opportunities beyond my wildest dreams. Marnie and Patti, you continue to support me and introduce me to wonderful connections and opportunities with so much encouragement and support. And to all the tech assistants who have had to patiently work alongside my last-minute starts and ADHD moments, you are appreciated more than you know. PESI will always hold a deep-seated, sacred, loyal place in my heart.

Arielle—Getting to know you on this journey has been such a blessing. You inspire me every time we have the opportunity to work together. Thank you for being a mentor, guide, example, and colleague. And thank you for your beautifully written foreword and willingness to contribute to this work. I am glad your Joel led us to the same path. It is an honor.

Rosemary—Your diligent and ongoing work with me throughout the last decade has ultimately been the catalyst that has allowed me to achieve the unthinkable—a life full of potential and opportunity. You have been my shelter amidst the storms of life and given me the hope necessary to keep moving forward. Thank you for being my guide. I am forever grateful.

Dani—I am not sure that anything in my life would be possible without you. You are the most genuine, loving person I know and have held me, laughed with me, cried with me, and continually challenged me to be the best version of myself along this journey. You were my life raft during this project.

Anna and Jack—Someday, I hope you get to read this book and know that you are capable of living beyond any dreams you may ever have. Never give up on people, and remember that healing is always possible. You are both truly the grace and love I never thought I deserved.

Bri and Steph—Truly, what would I do without you? I am so glad we are on this wild ride of life together. Through tears, laughs, and more, I can always count on you both to be there. The ongoing support, love, and encouragement during this project are not out of character for either of you. I love you both; you are my family.

Ben—I love you beyond words. You have been one of the greatest blessings in my life. Like Kylo Ren and Rey, the bond and love that I hold for you is sacred and will never change.

Mom—From as early as I remember, you have taught me how to work hard, pursue dreams, and make a difference in the world. Thank you for leading by example and showing me that being a working woman and helping those in need is invaluable.

Dad—All my most unique gifts and traits undoubtedly came from you. You have taught me the gift of creativity and shown me how to selflessly give to others, embrace life, and live to the fullest.

Jen—We have been on the same crazy life journey and are the only two people in the world who understand the struggles and pain we each have faced. I love you dearly. Your continued patience, unconditional love, and support, no matter what, are deeply cherished.

My Homie—This book was no doubt of your making and divine guidance. Thank you for entrusting me to help others, to see others, and to be authentically, messy, imperfect me. I owe you a life of service.

Bridget—I am so grateful for your patient, loving guidance along this writing journey. Your mentorship and knowledge are so valuable to me. Thank you for all the direction, support, and ongoing push you give me and so many others. I hope to be one ounce of the writer and person you are.

Ira—The wonderful world of EMDR would not have been made known to me if it were not for you. Your teaching, consultation, and ongoing leadership led me to forming my own love for EMDR. Thank you for inspiring and teaching me the way you have.

And last but not least, my team at New Harbinger. You all have gently guided me, redirected me, taught me, and been so dependable and encouraging throughout this process. This project has been challenging, yet you all always made it seem easy and doable. Thank you for the faith in me to carry this out as well as the endless support.

References

Brown, B. 2010. *The Gifts of Imperfection: Let Go of Who You Think You're Supposed to Be and Embrace Who You Are.* Center City, MN: Hazelden.

Centers for Disease Control and Prevention. 2019. "Adverse Childhood Experiences." https://www.cdc.gov/violenceprevention/aces/index.html

Eye Movement Desensitization and Reprocessing International Association. 2022. "What Is EMDR Therapy?" https://www.emdria.org/about-emdr-therapy

National Center for Injury Prevention and Control, Division of Violence Provision. 2021. "Adverse Childhood Experiences (ACEs), Substance Use, & Suicide: Opportunities for Public Health Prevention." https://www.ncsl.org/Portals/1/Documents/Health/CJones MCHFellows_34936.pdf

Parnell, L. 2018. *Rewiring the Addicted Brain with EMDR-Based Treatment.* Green Tara Books.

Shapiro, F. 2018. *Eye Movement Desensitization and Reprocessing (EMDR) Therapy: Basic Principles, Protocols, and Procedures.* 2nd ed. New York: Guilford Press.

van der Kolk, B. 2014. *The Body Keeps the Score: Brain, Mind, and Body in the Healing of Trauma.* New York: Viking.

Megan Salar, LCSW, ACADC, CCTP-II, EMDR-C, is a licensed clinical social worker who specializes in treating trauma and addiction. She owns and operates her own clinical practice, and provides supervision and consultation nationally and internationally to clinicians and businesses seeking ongoing trauma training. She provides clinical training in eye movement desensitization and reprocessing (EMDR), trauma, and addiction to mental and behavioral health professionals throughout the world, and is a proud training member of the PESI and Evergreen Certification family. She is a certified EMDR and CCTP II clinician, as well as an EMDR and CCTP II trainer and consultant through PESI and Evergreen Certifications. Megan also serves as an expert witness at the State and Federal level for her expertise in areas surrounding trauma.

Foreword writer **Arielle Schwartz, PhD,** is a licensed clinical psychologist, EMDR therapy consultant, and certified yoga instructor with a private practice in Boulder, CO. She is author of *The Complex PTSD Workbook* and *The Post-Traumatic Growth Guidebook,* and coauthor of *EMDR Therapy and Somatic Psychology.*

Real change *is* possible

For more than forty-five years, New Harbinger has published proven-effective self-help books and pioneering workbooks to help readers of all ages and backgrounds improve mental health and well-being, and achieve lasting personal growth. In addition, our spirituality books offer profound guidance for deepening awareness and cultivating healing, self-discovery, and fulfillment.

Founded by psychologist Matthew McKay and Patrick Fanning, New Harbinger is proud to be an independent, employee-owned company. Our books reflect our core values of integrity, innovation, commitment, sustainability, compassion, and trust. Written by leaders in the field and recommended by therapists worldwide, New Harbinger books are practical, accessible, and provide real tools for real change.

 **newharbinger**publications

MORE BOOKS from
NEW HARBINGER PUBLICATIONS

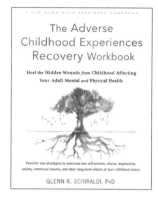

THE ADVERSE CHILDHOOD EXPERIENCES RECOVERY WORKBOOK

Heal the Hidden Wounds from Childhood Affecting Your Adult Mental and Physical Health

978-1684036646 / US $24.95

THE ANXIETY AND DEPRESSION WORKBOOK

Simple, Effective CBT Techniques to Manage Moods and Feel Better Now

978-1684036141 / US $24.95

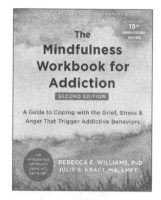

THE MINDFULNESS WORKBOOK FOR ADDICTION, SECOND EDITION

A Guide to Coping with the Grief, Stress, and Anger That Trigger Addictive Behaviors

978-1684038107 / US $24.95

THE DIALECTICAL BEHAVIOR THERAPY SKILLS WORKBOOK, SECOND EDITION

Practical DBT Exercises for Learning Mindfulness, Interpersonal Effectiveness, Emotion Regulation, and Distress Tolerance

978-1684034581 / US $24.95

THE SUICIDAL THOUGHTS WORKBOOK

CBT Skills to Reduce Emotional Pain, Increase Hope, and Prevent Suicide

978-1684037025 / US $21.95

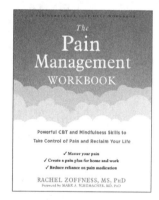

THE PAIN MANAGEMENT WORKBOOK

Powerful CBT and Mindfulness Skills to Take Control of Pain and Reclaim Your Life

978-1684036448 / US $24.95

newharbingerpublications

1-800-748-6273 / newharbinger.com

(VISA, MC, AMEX / prices subject to change without notice)

Follow Us 🄾 f 🅈 ▶ 🄾 🄿 in

Don't miss out on new books from New Harbinger.
Subscribe to our email list at **newharbinger.com/subscribe**

Did you know there are **free tools** you can download for this book?

Free tools are things like **worksheets, guided meditation exercises**, and **more** that will help you get the most out of your book.

You can download free tools for this book—whether you bought or borrowed it, in any format, from any source—from the New Harbinger website. All you need is a NewHarbinger.com account. Just use the URL provided in this book to view the free tools that are available for it. Then, click on the "download" button for the free tool you want, and follow the prompts that appear to log in to your NewHarbinger.com account and download the material.

You can also save the free tools for this book to your **Free Tools Library** so you can access them again anytime, just by logging in to your account! Just look for this button on the book's free tools page. ➔ **+ Save this to my free tools library**

If you need help accessing or downloading free tools, visit **newharbinger.com/faq** or contact us at **customerservice@newharbinger.com**.